CONVERSATIONS WITH
JOHN SCHLESINGER

RANDOM HOUSE TRADE PAPERBACKS

NEW YORK

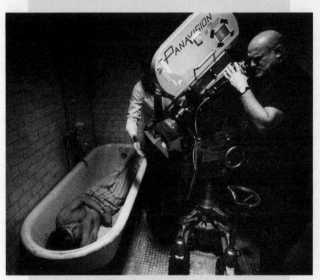

CONVERSATIONS WITH

John Schlesinger

Ian Buruma

A Random House Trade Paperback Original

Published in the United States by Random House Trade Paperbacks,
an imprint of The Random House Publishing Group, a division of
Random House, Inc., New York.

RANDOM HOUSE TRADE PAPERBACKS and colophon
are trademarks of Random House, Inc.

LIBRARY OF CONGRESS CATALOGING-IN-PUBLICATION DATA
Schlesinger, John, 1926–2003
Conversations with John Schlesinger / Ian Buruma.
p. cm.
ISBN 0-375-75763-5
1. Schlesinger, John, 1926—Interviews.   2. Motion picture producers and
directors—Great Britain—Interviews.   I. Buruma, Ian.   II. Title.
PN1998.3.S35A3 2006
791.4302'33'092—dc22   2005044350

Printed in the United States of America

www.atrandom.com

2 4 6 8 9 7 5 3 1

Book design by Casey Hampton

For Isabel

CONTENTS

INTRODUCTION

J ohn Schlesinger, born in London in 1926, was my mother's elder brother. My grandparents, the children of German-Jewish immigrants, were in many ways typical of their class in the north London borough of Hampstead: cultivated, musical, comfortably well-off, and highly assimilated in their corner of British society. The arts were taken seriously. All their five children were required to play a musical instrument and, if possible, become very good at it. John played the piano but failed to shine. Perhaps his early childhood ambition to become a cinema organist came out of this. He was mesmerized by those glamorous figures, bathed in light, who rose from and then descended into the orchestra pit on a hydraulic lift before the main entertainment.

John was the ideal bachelor uncle, ready to share stories and jokes even with the youngest family members, which made us feel included in a kind of conspiracy of fun. My earliest memories of him were of his conjuring tricks and his imitations of sinister German accents or the queen of Holland. The conspiracies of fun, when I grew up, mostly took place in St. Mary Woodlands House, my grandparents' old vicarage in rural Berkshire, where the family gathered for weekends and holidays. Later, they continued in a more adult fashion in London, L.A., New York, Delhi, Tokyo, or wherever our paths happened to cross, which was often.

I suppose I must have been aware that John was an artist from a very early age. Apart from doing conjuring tricks, he spent a lot of time, inside the house and out, taking photographs of us with his Rolleiflex. Some of these pictures—of me, raking the leaves, aged about five, fully nude—show a now almost quaint lack of inhibition, which would surely be frowned upon in our more puritanical times.

John received the kind of education that most members of the British upper-middle class have had to endure: private boarding schools from the age of eight and an endless regime of cold baths and games. No good at sports, John hated his time at an institution that prized sportsmanship as the highest masculine virtue. His father had hoped the school would make a man of him. Perhaps in a way it did. John told me that his homosexual inclinations were the one thing that put him in the mainstream of school life.

This was followed by more than two years in the army, for which he was as unsuited as he was for life at a spartan boarding school. But he found respite in the entertainment division, where his talent for conjuring and directing bawdy reviews, featuring drag acts and the like, made him feel more appreciated. His first real taste of serious drama, however, came at Oxford University, where he read English literature at Balliol College from 1947. Though hardly cut out for scholarship, he got valuable theatrical experience as an actor and director in the Oxford University Dramatic Society.

It was also while at Oxford that John made his first film, *Black Legend* (1948), together with his friend Alan Cooke. With money from his grandmother, they got family and friends to act in the dramatization of a seventeenth-century case of adultery and murder. This film, already shot through with John's dark sense of humor, was technically accomplished enough to be shown to Dylis Powell, the *Sunday Times* film critic, who spotted an unusual talent and praised the directors' enterprise.

After university, John started out as an actor, with modest success. We saw him on television once in a while, usually in small parts: a German sailor in a forgotten war movie by Michael Powell about the sinking of the *Graf Spee* (with Peter Finch as the captain); a horse thief in *Ivanhoe* (starring a roguish Roger Moore in tights), one of Robin Hood's Merry Men; and more in that same vein. He was a bit of a ham, which appealed to us children, but might have hampered his career as an actor.

John rather cherished his memories of playing dames in Christmas pantomimes. I cannot recall seeing him in any of these roles, but I have been told that he appeared as a dame on the night I was born. This performance in December 1951 took place in a provincial theater with a leaking roof. Family lore has it that the rain came pelting down on the pianist, a French friend of John's, but this is by the by.

I can remember, albeit with extreme vagueness, the first time I saw John making a film, because I was in it, with my sister, Ann. I have a photograph from this short film, entitled *Sunday in the Park*. It shows me, aged about four, pushing my sister through Kensington Gardens in a pram. This film, shown on BBC Television, was considered a failure by John, who never wanted it to be seen again.

In a sense, whether he was making a film or not, one always felt a little as if one were performing for John. He liked to be entertained, amused, stimulated. One soon knew when he was not, for his mind would drift off to somewhere far away—a script, a story idea, a fantasy, often (as he confided to me much later in life) to do with sex. Perhaps this, more than the Rollei or the magic wand, was the main sign of his artistic temperament. He would be there, listening, smiling, watching, and yet he *wasn't* always there. Not that much escaped his attention, or his gaze, but he had the art of taking everything in without necessarily listening. It was as if he soaked up life around him, almost by osmosis, like some watchful animal. If something struck him as particularly entertaining, he would snap it up like a juicy morsel for his private delectation, to be regurgitated at some later date, in a movie perhaps or simply as a story to be retold for the amusement of others. One always longed to be the producer of such juicy morsels. One seldom succeeded.

Even though I vaguely remember the shooting of *Sunday in the Park*, it was too early to think of my uncle as a film director. I was too young and John too new in his chosen career. His first real success as a filmmaker came with *Terminus* in 1961, a documentary about Waterloo Station. Aside from *Sunday in the Park*, he had already directed short documentaries for BBC Television and worked as a second-unit director on feature films, but *Terminus* was made for the cinema and won the Golden Lion award at the Venice Film Festival. This was the true launching pad of his career as a film director. The following year, the producer Joseph Janni asked him to direct *A Kind of Loving*, starring Alan Bates. It won the Golden Bear in Berlin.

Written by Keith Waterhouse and Willis Hall, *A Kind of Loving* was part of the British new wave of films and plays about the working class, mostly set in the industrial north, known as kitchen-sink drama. John, whose own milieu was as far removed from this world of rebellious miners' sons as it was from the lounge lizards and pipe-smoking RAF aces that dominated British cinema and stage before, tagged on to the kitchen-sink school without the leftist political convictions of some of his peers, such as Lindsay Anderson and Tony Richardson. Instead, he gave these gritty stories a humanist touch, somewhat akin to the Italian neorealists. John always stressed to me how much he loved "human" films: Truffaut, Satyajit Ray, Kurosawa, and De Sica were his heroes. This idea of humanity was often dismissed by his kitchen-sink colleagues as wishy-washy bourgeois liberalism. But it is precisely what gave such films as *A Kind of Loving* and *Billy Liar* (1963) their staying power.

We visited John on the set of *A Kind of Loving* and were shown around Shepperton Studios by a kind assistant. Several movies were in production at the time. I recall seeing a war film being shot: toy ships in a water tank approaching a painted backdrop of the Normandy beaches on D-day. There was also something called *It's Trad, Dad!*: young people sitting on a wall in jeans and sneakers snapping their fingers to a Dixieland band.

The set of *A Kind of Loving*, to a ten-year-old boy, was not very thrilling. In the middle of a vast movie studio was the interior of a working class dwelling in the north of England. Thora Hird played Alan Bates's shrewish mother-in-law. Bates's character felt trapped in a marriage to her daughter, played by June Ritchie. He particularly resented having to live in the same house as his mother-in-law. Thora Hird kept repeating, take after take, that he was now a married man and had to make sacrifices.

Watching a movie scene being shot, with the interminable delays—camera setups being tried, lights fixed, makeup adjusted, actors talked to, continuity girls consulted, gofers barked at, and so on and on—is never much fun. But it was exciting to see my uncle shout "Action!" and "Cut!" He was a commanding presence on the set, with a rather short fuse. I always suspected that he quite enjoyed his rages. Some hapless person usually had to bear the brunt. But mostly he seemed to direct in the way he spoke to us children, coaxing a performance out of people by making them laugh. When the scene was finally in the can, he would come over and introduce us to the stars. This was something that might have given him more pleasure than it did us, or indeed the stars. I learned to get used to the polite smiles and glazed looks of movie people holding out their hands to greet the relatives, but these would remain slightly awkward encounters. Watching Tom Courtenay do Hitler imitations at our family Christmas table was a different matter. And I do remember being shown around the studio with my grandmother once by a young American actor with time on his hands. He treated my grandmother as though she were the most beautiful young woman in the world. His name was Warren Beatty. Still, a movie set is not really a place for outsiders, however closely related to the director.

A Kind of Loving was not the last time I saw John on a set, however. On one occasion I appeared as an extra in a Bar Mitzvah in *Sunday Bloody Sunday*, shot at the Café Royal in London. Not that I'm very visible: a face in a crowd, applauding as the food is wheeled in on great silver platters. The other extras were almost all Jews, specializing in playing Jewish types. Some were Holocaust survivors, who spoke bitterly about the *goyim* during the lunch break. But this was much more satisfying than just hanging out. I was getting interested in the mechanics of making a film. There were no stars to be presented to this time. John was too busy, and I was not his nephew but a paid extra.

Sunday Bloody Sunday is John's most personal film. He certainly considered it one of his best. The main character, a gay Jewish doctor, played by Peter Finch, was in many ways close to John himself: unashamed of his sexual preference, a lover of classical music (especially opera), funny, unconventional, yet deeply loyal both to his lover, who hardly merits it, and to his family. John was the same. A certain clannishness was perhaps the main remnant of our Jewish past. Indeed, as someone—I cannot remember whom—once said of his own assimilated family, our Jewishness showed itself in our excessive passion for celebrating Christmas: no church, much food, big presents. John did sometimes go to the synagogue on high holidays, but again, I believe, mainly out of loyalty to a tradition that he cherished.

There are, of course, bits of John in many of his films: the recurrence of his worst fears, often going back to his childhood—trapped birds, rats, sudden acts of brutality. But more than violence, which he deeply feared, it was human love, in its many varieties, that inspired his best work. He regretted at the end of his life that he had not expressed his own sexuality more openly in his films. He was always looking for gay subjects but was too good an artist to take them up for the sake of a social or political cause. Though proud to have come out, he would have hated to be pinned down as a "gay director."

Nonetheless, a certain homosexual sensibility, if one can call it that, does come through in such films as *Midnight Cowboy*, which celebrates the love between two men trapped in a hostile world of rapacious or coldhearted women. Not that these two drifters, Joe Buck, the phony cowboy, and Ratso Rizzo, the consumptive bum, ever have sex together or express the slightest desire to do so. And the few glimpses we get of homosexual activity—a furtive blowjob in an all-night cinema and a sordid pickup, ending in an act of terrifying violence—are far from celebratory. This has been read by more politically minded figures than John as "coyness" or a kind of furtive apologia. But the point here was not to advertise a sexual preference; these grim scenes were part of life in the big city. Love, in John's films, is not bound by categories or classifications.

If John had a philosophy in life, it was his belief in loyalty. This is not the same as sexual fidelity, which to him was far from absolute. He was not a moralist. The pursed lips of disapproval were something he abhorred. But he had a clear vision of how people are led astray by their illusions. A realist, more than a romantic, he saw the need for compromise. The doctor in *Sunday Bloody Sunday* is resigned to sharing his feckless lover with another person, if that is all he can get: half a loaf is still better than no loaf at all. Billy Liar is content to be a dreamer in his north-country town and not leave his family for the bright city lights. Always thinking there is someone around the corner—someone richer, more famous, more glamorous than her current lover—is the downfall of Diana, the young model played by Julie Christie in *Darling*. After dreaming of taking New York by storm as a hustler, the Midnight Cowboy settles for his friendship with another loser on skid row. The tawdry illusions of Hollywood glamour are what attracted John to Nathanael West's *The Day of the Locust*. That he was not immune to these illusions himself only sharpened the fascination.

John's love-hate affair with the United States marked his career, as well as his private life. His partner, Michael Childers, was an American who was happier in New York or California than in London. John was both inspired and appalled by America. He never wanted to be a full-time resident in the United States and remained loyal to England, which he regarded with great affection and almost constant irritation. He loved the English landscape, celebrated in his adaptation of Thomas Hardy's *Far from the Madding Crowd* (1967), and cherished many British institutions, including the royal family. He shared with others of his generation an odd veneration for the Queen Mother. But he loathed the narrow horizons of English life, the attitude of "Oh, no, we couldn't possibly do that. That's not the way we do things here."

What attracted him to America was the opposite: its openness and enthusiasm. Though a traditionalist at heart, he was excited by the fluid, rootless, can-do aspects of American life. Yet he often expressed his distaste for what he saw as "the wrong values"—the horror of failure, the worship of money, the fickleness of human ties; he sometimes complained that some of his American friends melted away after he had made a flop. He felt "safer" in England and at the same time constrained and not always sufficiently appreciated. Even as he prized the good-humored loyalty of his British crews, he resented the cash-strapped, penny-pinching way of making films in Britain. He liked a grander stage.

And so he kept returning to the United States, hooked by its energy and excitement, hoping to repeat the huge success of *Midnight Cowboy*. But times had changed since 1969. John was unsuited to the age of blockbusters and feel-good films, chasing after an ever-younger audience. He made some decent thrillers: *Marathon Man* (1976), *The Falcon and the Snowman* (1985), *Pacific Heights* (1990). He also made the much-underrated *The Day of the Locust* (1975), which he himself cherished, partly perhaps because of its bruised reputation.

However American the subject of his films, John always retained an Englishman's eye, which enriched his work but had its drawbacks, too. He saw the dark humor of the American scene and gave it a sophisticated edge, but a supercilious European disdain could sometimes make his satire go over the top, as in the great flop of his career, a screwball comedy about hucksterism in small-town Florida entitled *Honky Tonk Freeway* (1981).

Despite some notable American successes, I believe John's best films were set in England. There he could be satirical without condescension. Just as Robert Altman's acid views of America are tempered by love, John's attachment to his native country stayed his heavy-handed tendencies. This shows in some of his late films, such as *Cold Comfort Farm* (1995), and especially in *An Englishman Abroad* (1983) and *A Question of Attribution* (1992), two short films about Guy Burgess and Anthony Blunt, written by Alan Bennett for the BBC. John's (and Bennett's) take on the two gay Englishmen who spied for the Soviet Union is compassionate without being sentimental about what they did. In a way, Burgess and Blunt fit perfectly in John's long line of misfits, very British even at the heart of the British establishment and at the same time on the outside, dreaming of a fantasy world where they might be heroes: Billy Liars spying for Stalin.

Although chiefly known as a film director, John no more wished to be pinned down as a filmmaker than as a "gay director." He did theater productions through much of his career, from *Timon of Athens* for the Royal Shakespeare Company in 1965 to Sam Shepherd's *True West* in 1981. But his greatest love was opera. "No more Shakespeare without music" was one of his mottos later in life, perhaps because he always found producing Shakespeare rather daunting.

John's most successful opera production was of Offenbach's *Les contes de Hoffmann,* with Placido Domingo, first performed at Covent Garden in 1980. He also produced Verdi's *Un Ballo in Maschera* for the Salzburg Festival in 1989, just before its director, Herbert von Karajan, died. John rather dreaded working with Karajan, the kind of German (authoritarian, pro-Nazi during the war) he liked to hate. But in fact, they got along fine. Karajan's spiky wit appealed to John. Their oddly successful relationship also illustrates another aspect of John: his absolute belief in the supremacy of art and especially music.

I often asked him about the—to me—incongruous fact that the Schlesinger family happily traveled to Bayreuth in 1951 for the first Wagner festival after the war. John, like many Jews who survived at a relatively safe distance from the killing grounds of the Third Reich, had a thing about Germany and Germans. He disliked working there and eagerly admitted to being deeply prejudiced about a people he regarded as humorless and congenitally prone to cruelty. And yet, when it came to Wagner or Leni Riefenstahl's mastery of film or Herbert von Karajan, all prejudice vanished in a haze of artistic admiration. Great art, for him, transcended politics and other worldly concerns. In this, he was a product of his cultivated Anglo-German-Jewish ancestry. His grandfather Richard Schlesinger, who came over to England from Frankfurt in the 1880s, was an orthodox Jew with a passion for Wagner's operas—not at all, it must be added, an oddity for his time and generation.

The last time I visited John on a movie set, we had lunch in Cecil B. DeMille's old garden in Beverly Hills. John was already at the end of his tether, recovering from heart surgery and suffering from serious diabetes. He was working on his last, ill-fated film, entitled *The Next Best Thing* (2000), a movie he should never have made, starring Rupert Everett and Madonna. But it was a "gay subject," had the air of Hollywood glamour, and offered a faint promise of letting him go out with a bang. The stars met the relative: Madonna held out a drooping wrist and murmured *enchantée;* Rupert Everett sulked; and Gavin Lambert, the well-known writer, cast as an extra in the film, appeared on the set in a splendid wig, carrying a birthday cake.

It was round about this time that John and I decided to have a taped "conversation" about his life. We had discussed books before. John had talked about writing a memoir, and had even read bits of it into a Dictaphone. But nothing came of that. John was not a great reader and even less of a writer. He had neither the patience nor the confidence. I was never sure why. John was a highly educated man who spoke beautiful English. But he had a lifelong thing about not being "intellectual." Intellectuals, he often said, made him feel uncomfortable, even inadequate. Again, I'm not entirely sure why. Our family is well-read and cultivated in music and the arts, but there was never any great pressure to be highbrow. My grandmother was the closest thing to being an intellectual (she read German at Oxford), and her elder brother, Walter, was highbrow to a fault. (His many children were not allowed to play with anything so vulgar as a football.) John doted on his mother, Win, and rather liked his crusty Uncle Walter. If John failed at anything in life, it was not in literary but in sporting pursuits. And yet he felt ill at ease with intellectuals or "literary people," and that was that. Possibly it had something to do with his artistic temperament, the soaking up of impressions by instinct rather than intellect. Whatever the reason, he never felt able to write up his own life.

Since I passed, in John's eyes, for a dreaded "intellectual," he rather hoped I would write the book for him. This, rightly or wrongly, I was disinclined to do. I certainly had no interest in becoming his ghost, and I hesitated to write his biography. In a way I felt that anything I wrote about him would also be about myself, and I lacked the objective eye, the necessary sliver of ice, to be his biographer. And that is why, inspired partly by Cameron Crowe's brilliant book on Billy Wilder, we decided on a conversation.

We would do the kind of thing so many people regret not having done when their parents die, and their stories die with them. We would sit down and talk, as he put it, "with no holds barred," about his life as a man and a filmmaker. It worked, I believe, precisely because he was my uncle and not my father. I was not necessarily closer to him than to my father, but close in a different way. It is hard to discuss, say, the sexual life of one's parents. With John, this never had been a problem. He had always been open about his life and loves, even when I was still at an age when knowingness had to substitute for experience. John was always generous about sharing his life—not only by introducing the stars but by discussing his worries, his hopes, his disappointments, as though we were all part of the plot.

And in a way we were. For we took pride in his achievements, as though they rubbed off a little on us. My sister and

I still discuss his work as a kind of a family affair. There was a time when I even tried to emulate him. My decision to study film was no doubt inspired by his example—and perhaps was even another attempt to hold his interest. The fact that I went to film school in Tokyo was an eccentricity that appealed to him more than my chosen subject. I don't think he saw film as something to be studied—that was for "intellectuals."

To be boring was the worst sin in John's book. He made some bad films, but he was never boring, not even in his worst movies, embarked upon for the sake of money or staying on the job. He could not bear to be idle or bored. Life, for him, revolved around "the three Fs": films, fucks, and food—not necessarily in that order. One by one, the Fs deserted him, and it was then that he was ready, and had the time, to sit down with me and a tape recorder. We talked in Strawberry Hole, his country house in Sussex, in his apartment on the Gloucester Road in London, and at his other country retreat, in Palm Springs, California.

The conversations, cut off in the end by a massive stroke, cover most of his films. They certainly include the ones he felt most strongly about. When the subject of his last film, with Madonna, came up, he would sigh and say we would get round to more about that later. Alas, we never did. Editing the tapes, after his death in 2003, has been a fascinating and rather melancholy task. I still heard his voice in my head long after he was gone. I hope this comes through on the page as well, even to those who did not know him. Here it is, then, John Schlesinger, no holds barred.

CONVERSATIONS WITH
JOHN SCHLESINGER

CHILDHOOD

John Schlesinger was the son of a pediatrician and an accomplished violinist. Three of his grandparents were immigrants from Germany. One of his grandmothers was born in Manchester. Before going to St. Edmund's, a preparatory school in Surrey, he attended the Hall School in London. After St. Edmund's he spent five years at Uppingham in Rutland.

Let's start at the beginning. Your first memory of theater or film.

The first theater I ever saw was of two famous magicians, called Maskelyne and Devant. My father took me to see them, and I became fascinated by magic. There were big stage illusions which in one way or another have continued to be popular with magicians ever since, probably using the same principles. I loved the show and thought that one of

the things, apart from a cinema organist, that I would like to
be was a stage magician, and I took it up very keenly.

A cinema organist?

Yes, the image of a purple spotlight on the cinema organist, as he waves and then sinks with his organ down into the
bowels of the earth, was always rather special. When I was
eleven, I read in a magazine about the Paris Exhibition, and
there was an organ which played colored waterfalls—you
know, waterspouts. My father took me to Paris to see it. I went
to the restaurant where you could play this organ and see the
colored fountains. It was all terribly glamorous. I was really
quite serious about learning to play the organ and indeed did so
at the West London Synagogue. I had lessons, and at boarding
school—my prep school—I used to play the organ in chapel.

It was only a two-manual organ, not more complicated
than that, and I can't say that I listen avidly now to organ
recitals, but it started me off being interested in music,
which became a very important part of my life.

*I suppose the organ, particularly in a church, though per-
haps not in the West London Synagogue so much, was also
part of the drama of religion. Was that part of the attraction? Was there a magical quality about being in a chapel,
the chanting and so on?*

Maybe. My first sexual experience was linked to my
playing the organ at school. We were changing to go horse

riding one day, and another boy beckoned me over to the cubicle he was changing in. And I suppose one could say that we fiddled—not much more than that. That night I was playing the organ in chapel and when I pulled out the stops to start playing whatever hymn it was, there was a terrible kind of subterranean noise, which went like *eeeeeeer,* and I thought, What on earth is this? and pushed all the stops in to try and stop it, and then they announced the hymn ancient and modern number, and I pulled the stops out again— *eeeeeeer.* I thought, Oh, my God! This is a visitation, this is because of something terribly wrong that I have done, and I'm being punished for it. Anyhow, it was a rather embarrassing service, because I couldn't stop this noise. In the end I realized that it was a pure accident. My cassock had got caught on one of the pedals, which caused this noise to happen, and guilt vanished—forever, I think—as a result of that.

How old were you when this happened?

Eleven, I suppose.

Apart from cinema organs and magic shows, what other theater did you see as a child?

I can remember going to *Peter Pan.* We saw Charles Laughton playing the parts of Mr. Darling and Captain Hook. And Jean Forbes-Robertson was the perennial Peter—she was said to have gin hidden in her wig box. But it was wonderful. These were special occasions, on my grandmothers' birthdays and in the Christmas holidays. The first opera I ever saw was *Hansel and Gretel*, which is still musically one of my favorite pieces. I didn't get to work in the opera—and never thought I would—until very much later. But I remember my parents saying good night to us when they were off to the opera in full evening dress—tailcoat, et cetera.

You see, there was a glamour to the theater. I always remember wondering what was behind the curtain in the days they had curtains in the theater. They don't so often now. You know, you see a dimly lit set when you walk into the theater. I sometimes think that's rather a pity—I like the surprise of the curtain going up, revealing what's behind it.

The magic . . .

Yes.

When did you start doing your own shows?

Quite early on. We used to celebrate birthdays and that kind of thing by doing our own shows. My parents—your grandparents—were very encouraging about our doing things for ourselves, making things for ourselves. Anything we made was considered important—including our own entertainment. And so it became a custom to put on shows for my grandmothers' birthdays and other such occasions. We usually imitated them and were probably very rude about everybody, but the family shows became a great standby, and we were allowed to make a total mess of the dining room—putting up dust sheets for curtains and all that kind of thing, because I was always interested in presentation. If I was having a film show, I always had colored lights on the screen, got hold of a dimmer of some sort, and could present something as a performance. I've always been interested in that.

And the movies? What was the first film you saw?

I remember being taken to the Tatler cinema, which used to exist on Tottenham Court Road, and seeing a full-length documentary about the war between China and Japan. It was called *China and Japan*, but I can't remember the details of it.

Later on, I saw films at my prep school, St. Edmund's, in Surrey. This was in the thirties, when there was a great deal of publicity about Germany and the growing Nazi influence, and German expressionistic films were the fashion. So one of the first films I remember seeing was *The Cabinet of Dr. Caligari*. We had a wonderful schoolmaster, who was very keen on German expressionism and arranged for us to see the films he considered important and we didn't really appreciate.

How old were you then?

Between nine and thirteen. I remember *The Last Laugh* being shown, and we didn't appreciate it at all.

Did you see M?

I didn't see *M*. It was considered to be too strong for us.

This was after you got your first camera?

I was about nine when I got my first camera, I think, from my grandmother. She didn't want for a quarter of tea, since my grandfather was a very successful stockbroker. They lived in a big house on Fitzjohns Avenue, which was nicknamed Fitzjews Avenue in those days. I was at the Hall, Hampstead, as a day boy and used to go and visit her quite often from school. My grandfather, who had been a very active man, was suffering badly from Parkinson's disease and dribbled terribly, so he had a sort of bib permanently on and could only speak in a whisper, which was terrifying to me.

I first used my camera for "granny in the back garden" kind of films. But I did make a film of our prep school, which began with an invisible hand opening the front gate, as if by magic. There was a sequence in this film of the school being taken away to the seaside for the day and rather intimate shots of the headmaster, Mr. Bully, changing under his towel. This was considered infra dig, so they tried to prevent me from including it in the film.

Was this kind of thing encouraged at school? I had always heard you were a very unhappy schoolboy.

I didn't like games. I wasn't good at it, and that was one of my problems at school. I never felt I was appreciated for the positive things I could do. I was very good at drawing and designing posters for the school play, but games were considered to be important above everything else. And I was always scared of physical things. My father had been at the same public school—Uppingham—and when I went there, aged thirteen, I was haunted by the image of him in a school photograph of the rugby team or whatever it was. My brother, who was junior to me when he came to school, was also very good at games. He was more in the mold of my father. I always felt that I was never going to do that well because of this discrepancy. My parents knew I was not happy at school and that I was bullied, but they just thought, you know, you've got to rise above this and endure whatever happens and stick at school. I was always wanting to run away.

This is important, since many of your films are about people who are dreamers or outsiders or failures of one kind or another.

I knew I didn't fit in, and I regretted that terribly, and it probably informed everything in my life.

So that's a good thing, really, with hindsight. You might never have made films if you'd been a good sportsman.

Well, I don't know about that, but I wouldn't have harped to such an extent on the idea of failing in the eyes of other people. I've been dogged by that all my life. I'm very conscious now, years later, of being a product of a family that was acutely sensitive about this. I think that comes from my mother's side. My father was very optimistic and bullish and gung ho, and his motto, "Never take no for an answer," was something that I personally adopted and felt strongly about, but my mother was much more concerned about other people's opinions—what they thought of her. I remember when we were living in Berkshire during the war. She was a great gardener, and she wore what she considered very unattractive working clothes. One day she had to drive me to the station, which was a tiny place, and the only person she was likely to run into would be Lionel, the porter. She insisted on changing her clothes. I'd ask her why on earth she had to do that, and she said: "Well, I can't go in these gardening clothes, I must get out of them," and I said, "Who are you dressing for?" and she said, "Well, Lionel might see me."

Do you think that being from a family of immigrants made her more self-conscious?

I think it was entirely to do with her personality. I don't think it was anything that was premeditated. I remember being rather reluctant to perform at some impromptu concert at school. I was not a bad pianist, but I was told off for making too much fuss in refusing to appear because I didn't think I was good enough. They—not my parents but the school—said that was a form of boastfulness. So I never was quite sure how to play any form of success. I certainly played up failure, and I always have. Even when I've had good notices, I would say: "Oh yes, but this didn't work and that didn't work" and look on the negative side of things. That's been very much part of our family inheritance.

I still wonder whether there is not more to this than individual personality. I think it always comes back to the "Lionel" problem. As long as one has the feeling, even slightly, of being outsiders in a society, there is that nagging pressure to succeed a little bit better than other people in order to be appreciated. No?

Yes, yes. Particularly if one was not succeeding at something that was accepted as being the norm.

Being Jewish was never the issue?

I did know that being Jewish was in some ways a disadvantage, particularly if you were bullied as a result of it—and I was.

Yet the family was not very Jewish in its habits or customs.

I had a very strange religious upbringing. My father was rather egalitarian, in the sense that he thought any place of worship was as good as another. We used to go to the Liberal Jewish Synagogue—which we nicknamed "Cinemagogue"—on Saturdays. I remember one rather dramatic morning, when the rabbi, a much revered figure named Mattock, whom I used to call Dramattock, got up to preach and was stopped by a man who was clearly trying to interrupt the service. He probably had something to do with Oswald Mosley, the famous fascist at the time. This man wasn't allowed to continue and was escorted out. It was all very dramatic, and a sort of cloud came over the congregation. This realization that something out of the ordinary had happened was something that stayed with me. I tried to use this in the synagogue scene in *Sunday Bloody Sunday*. But it didn't really fit—a good idea which didn't work. But I can remember it as the first fascistic gesture I experienced.

You went every Saturday?

Not every Saturday, but we went during the school holidays quite often and certainly on high holidays. I'm the only member of the family that still retains, as it were, my Jewishness. I like my association with the Liberal Jewish Synagogue. I still go on high holidays.

Yet you never had a Bar Mitzvah?

No. I did not.

Why not?

Because my parents didn't think it was so important, I suppose. After all, any place of worship is as good as another. I've rather regretted it. I rather wish I'd had a more Jewish upbringing.

Was there an element of snobbery in your upbringing, in the sense that middle-class Anglo-Jews, especially of German-Jewish descent, were a cut above religious Jews from Russia and Poland—people who were less assimilated? Was it not considered slightly bad form to be too obviously Jewish?

I didn't think of it in that way at the time. I suppose there were occasions when one was embarrassed by unattractive Jewish qualities in other people. I remember a school friend, with whom I used to give film performances, after which we would ask people to contribute for a charity at the end. This friend of mine, whose name was John Lazarus, always used to say, in a rather thick Jewish accent: "Thank you for coming, and there's a box at the door." "There's a box at the door" became a sort of running gag.

I'm thinking more of your parents. My grandmother, especially, seemed to be hyperconscious of certain kinds of Jews, as she would put it, "giving Jews a bad name."

Well, one was certainly conscious of Jews getting a bad name, yes. Although I didn't think of it in those terms. I mean, it was much more personal to me. It was why they were chasing me at school. You know: "Let's chase Schlesinger!"

To turn back a little, what happened to the boy in the cubicle at school, with whom you had your first sexual experience? Was that ever repeated?

No, it never was. I mean, not with him. It got me interested, but funnily enough I ran into him much, much later. I didn't talk to him, but there he was at an art exhibition with his, presumably, then wife. And I recognized him—I don't know that he recognized me—and remembered that incident, which set me on the path, I suppose, of my sexuality, which didn't change. I knew from a fairly early age that my life was going to be sexually orientated toward homosexuality, and it's a very important part of my life.

How did that affect your life at school?

It was a very common thing when I was at public school. You know, a male society sleeping in a dormitory. It was very much part of one's life, and a very welcome part of life as far as I was concerned. I did have feelings of embarrassment, I suppose. I didn't like discussing it, or for people to think that was my way of life, but subsequently all that changed.

But it was accepted as part of school life?

Absolutely. I didn't have a feeling of guilt then. The feeling of guilt happened, funnily enough, much later. But it was a fairly common practice at school. I remember going to bed with someone who, I think, basically disliked me and bullied me. I don't know why I succumbed to any kind of sexual relationship with him, but I remember very clearly that I did, and that he was always apologizing for his behavior, but it didn't let up.

How old would you have been then?

Thirteen, fourteen.

The fear of violence and the fascination with it is very much part of your work. Do you think this goes back to your childhood experiences?

I think that it's in every child's nature. A lot of the games that one plays from early years—you know: "Bang, you're dead!" That's a fantasy which is perfectly all right and perfectly normal for everybody to play and I suppose I never considered it special, but it persisted—the macabre and my interest in it.

I remember that my grandmother had a taste for Hoffmann's Struwwelpeter *and other rather cruel German children's stories.*

Yes, that was part of the heritage. *Struwwelpeter* was certainly pretty cruel, and children loved and love it still. Yes, we liked that.

I've certainly used certain phobias in my films that I've had from an early age. For instance, my obsession with insects. The opening of *Eye for an Eye* shows a child who is terrified of a moth that's flying around. This is very personal to me, because I was always terrified of these fluttering things. I've also used my feelings about spiders and cockroaches. You do use, I think, things that scare one—darkness, sudden surprises. None of this is out of the ordinary. But they are things that I've reacted to adversely in my life, and the fact that I've used violence in films is not because I like violence but that I'm scared of it.

Is this related to the war in any way?

Possibly. But things happen without your really understanding them or thinking about the ramifications. I've never been that analytical. You are used to that, because you are the writer that you are, and you've got that kind of mind. I don't have that, so I've never lived my life consciously attributing certain things to the results of something I've experienced or done. We all have prejudices, of course, and one of mine is a hatred of all things German, as a result of the Holocaust. But that only came much later, when the full horror of it became known and was discussed and written about frequently.

Going to Germany after the war and even working there, in Berlin on Ian McEwan's *The Innocent,* made me very conscious of my anti-German feelings. I never suffered personally at their hands, but I do remember a relative in Holland named Martin Schuster, who was in a wheelchair. Martin, who was much older than me, had the same birth date as I did and always used to remember my birthday. Then suddenly the birthday cards stopped. I heard subsequently that he had been sent to a concentration camp and was exterminated. I find it awfully difficult to divorce all that from my basic anti-German feelings. I mean I was ridiculous to the extent that for years I remember shopping in Hamleys, the famous toy shop in London, for Christmas and asking, "Where does this come from?" and if they said "Germany" I wouldn't have it, wouldn't touch it. It was ludicrous because I realized that I had a German camera and a German car.

And you, like all of us in the family, are a great lover of Wagner's music.

I don't think that matters. I can't really get hot under the collar because Wagner was espoused to such a great extent by Hitler. I can't say I couldn't bear to hear his music because of its associations.

Yes, but with Wagner it is about more than associations. He was violently anti-Semitic.

Yes, he was. So it is believed.

No, he wrote—

Yes, yes, he was. There is no question.

That's why his music was banned in Israel and even in Holland for a long time.

A mistake. I think art can't be treated like that. Years later, when I was going to do *Un Ballo in Maschera* for the Salzburg Festival with Herbert von Karajan, a Hollywood producer who was very Jewish said: "I can't understand how you can work with this man." I said to this producer that Karajan was a marvelous conducter and a great musician, implying that his Nazi past should be beneath consideration. You have to divorce the politics from music. And he said, "Well, I can't, and I don't know how you can," and I said "Well, I think one has to."

You used to see Leni Riefenstahl's movies at school. Would you say the same of her work for the Nazis, films such as Triumph of the Will?

I think one has to be able to see a piece of work in its own right and acknowledge her film as a brilliant piece of work and propaganda.

Can one really look at it purely from an aesthetic point of view, without thinking of the political context?

All I can say is that I've tried never to look at something and make the political aspect of it more important than the actual endeavor itself. I mean, *Triumph of the Will* is remarkable to look at, no question. I prefer to leave it at that, though I agree that if you start to examine it more thoroughly, there are other things that can sway you in a different direction.

Was there a moment or an event in your childhood that made you feel that you were an artist?

I was anxious for evidence that people thought I had something to offer, because I was so down in the mouth about not being good at the things that boys of sixteen and seventeen were supposed to be good at. When I was still at school and they were doing a play—I've forgotten what it was—I asked whether I could design the poster. When I did so and people said nice things about it, I thought: "Oh well, I've got something to offer—sort of." But it was a long, gradual process. When I began to feel confident in what I was capable of, when I felt I could say boo to a goose, it gave me a great sense of freedom.

You have said a lot about feeling inadequate at sports. But you have also often expressed a discomfort about intellectuals. Did that have anything to do with your mother's rather high intellectual expectations?

Well, she was a very intelligent, well-read woman, and I really didn't try to compete with all that. I've never regarded myself as an intellectual, though others may have done. I've always felt a bit deficient in that department. I'm not and never have been a great reader, which I regret. And chamber music—which is regarded as a rather intellectual appreciation—only came late into my life. I was accused at school of saying I liked it for show, which wasn't true. I genuinely thought it was too complicated and deep for me. I've always realized that I'm not really considered important as an artist, or that's what I thought, by the way I was judged. I've never been a critics' darling, but I've always been conscious of what people have been saying about me and my work. I worried about it. I've not been frightfully good at forging ahead without looking left or right, of which my father was capable. I've got better at it now, but it's taken a lot of experience and different kinds of work to get me to that point.

GETTING STARTED

After finishing at Uppingham school in 1944, John was called up for the army. He suffered from vertigo, had caught rheumatic fever, broke his leg, mislaid his gun, and failed to get a commission in the Royal Engineers. His best time in the army was in Singapore, where he was seconded as a conjurer into the Combined Services Entertainment Unit.

From 1947 to 1950, he studied English literature at Balliol College, Oxford, and joined the Oxford University Dramatic Society. Among other things, he performed in *The Tempest*, as Horatio in *Hamlet*, in Thomas Dekker's *The Shoemaker's Holiday*, and in a pageant for Princess Elizabeth, with the future critic Ken Tynan. Also while at Oxford, he made his first amateur films: *Black Legend* (1948) and *The Starfish* (1950).

John went on tours to France and the United States as an

actor with the Oxford Players. He got his professional start as an actor with the Colchester Repertory Theatre. He played in *Mourning Becomes Electra*, directed by Peter Hall. Lindsay Anderson directed an episode for television of *The Adventures of Robin Hood*, in which John played a minor part. His debut as a film actor was in Roy Boulting's *Single-Handed* (1953). In 1955, he acted in Michael Powell and Emeric Pressburger's *Oh... Rosalinda!!* He played the part of Dr. Goldfinger in Terence Fisher's *The Last Man to Hang?* (1956), and in that same year appeared in Powell and Pressburger's *The Battle of the River Plate*.

When you left school, how did your artistic interests develop? Were you still mainly interested in music or the theater?

All of them. I was interested in music and drama, designing. My first ambition professionally was to be a designer for film.

Why for film?

Because it had more basis in architectural truth, perhaps, and I read a lot. My literature in those days was all about design—Gordon Craig, and his son, Edward Carrick, whom I later worked with on a commercial. He had written a book about design and the cinema. So architecture was something that I thought I would pursue, since it's important, if you're going to be a designer for the cinema, to know about architectural design and construction. I wanted to go to the Architectural Association to study. Never did. But I became an architectural draftsman in the Royal Engineers, as well as a conjurer.

You were in the army between school and Oxford?

I was stationed up in Manchester as an architectural draftsman, and I would spend all my spare time at the Manchester Opera House or the Palace, Manchester, watching shows of different sorts. I was just as interested in the music hall as I was in the reconstituted Old Vic, where I saw Laurence Olivier and Ralph Richardson.

So, even though you had a camera and you made films at school, the ambition to be a filmmaker didn't come until later.

Being an architectural draftsman cured me of wanting to become an architect, because I designed loos most of the time. My job was designing latrines or drawing up latrines in Singapore, and I found that boring.

But weren't you also in the entertainment division?

Yes, I auditioned for a review with a speciality act doing conjuring tricks. I wasn't terribly good, but I enjoyed doing them, and it was an interesting group. The unit had as acting unpaid sergeants Stanley Baxter, Peter Nichols, the writer, and Kenneth Williams, who was honing his comic talents as that rather camp character that he subsequently played on radio and television. And there were some real showbiz people. Ivor Novello's old stage manager was in charge of the whole outfit, and he'd been in all those early musicals. The place was full of gossip and theatrical behavior.

What particular memories do you have of those days?

I remember seeing them all off on a train when they were going on tour to northern Malaysia, and there was a very outrageous character who had in civilian life been a worker at the Home Colonial Stores, patting butter—I remember that. Anyway, he turned up very late for the train, covered in bruises, and saying to us all: "Does it show, dear?" He'd applied some makeup, very badly, to try and hide the black eyes and things like that. He'd obviously been in some terrible trouble, and we had to adjust his makeup so that it wouldn't be quite so obvious that he'd been beaten up, presumably from some sexual advance or other. He was very amusing.

There is also a slightly sinister aspect to that story, which reminds me of a scene in one of your films, Madame Sousatzka, *I think, where a gay man gets beaten up in London.*

Oh yes, that was in *Sousatzka.*

How dangerous was homosexuality in the 1950s?

It was illegal. If you were caught having any kind of sexual—male sexual—experience, you could be in jail for it, and people did go to jail. The monstrosity of policemen dressed in civilian clothes standing in public lavatories and giving the come-on so that they could trap people making advances was known to happen and considered extraordinarily unfair. But the police did it, and people got caught that way.

What about the risk of getting beaten up if you picked up the wrong person?

I think the risk was much more being arrested in a public loo or in a park or wherever. It was something that we lived with. I've had friends and indeed relatives who've been arrested on suspicion of soliciting.

How long were you in the entertainment division?

Oh, not much more than six months. I felt at home there. But I didn't last long because I complained about prejudice toward us. There was a sergeant-major who was always picking on us or those who weren't a shining example of soldiering, and we felt picked on and uncomfortable. I was told that if I didn't like it, I could be returned to my old unit and go back to the drawing board. So I said, Very well, I'll apply for that, and they ripped off my acting unpaid sergeant's stripes and back I went to designing latrines. That sergeant-major, by the way, was caught embezzling and eventually committed suicide by taking cyanide in front of the whole sergeants' mess.

So you came out of the entertainment corps, went back to England—then what happened?

I went to university. Suddenly all those years—I was four years in the army—of having to toe the line were over, and I felt wonderfully free when I went up to Oxford and Balliol College and spent a blissful time acting and directing and not taking life too seriously. And I was rather good, I think, doing everything from reviews to classical plays.

I was in a very spectacular production of *The Tempest* in Worcester College Gardens, directed by a famous English literature professor named Nevil Coghill. I played Trinculo, one of the jesters. One of my lines was "Oh, I do smell all horse piss." At the end we sailed away in the boat, and Prospero had thrown his books into the lake, and Ariel had waved good-bye and then disappeared up in the trees in a blaze of fireworks. It was very beautiful, and we all came back to find our weeping friends and relatives, who had been very moved by the whole experience. One can't always sense the effect that one is having at the time. This is something that I have discovered quite often since. It always gives me great pleasure to realize that one has done something that contained more emotion than one thought.

Can you give me another example?

I can think of certain scenes in films that I've made. My first feature film was *A Kind of Loving,* the story of a young man who thinks he's in love with a woman, gets her pregnant, marries her—does the right thing—and suffers the indignity of having to live in the house with his mother-in-law, who's dead against the whole thing. There is a sequence when the young man turns up drunk and vomits all over the living room and then leaves, temporarily. It's sort of funny and moving, but I didn't realize the power of this scene until I saw how strongly the audience reacted to it. When that happens, and you realize the power that is at your fingertips for creating something that has high emotional impact, it's great, it's wonderful.

You don't know it when you're on the set and actually film-ing a scene like that? There are stories of famous scenes being shot, and everyone on the set being in tears. Does that happen rarely, in your experience?

First of all, you've expended all the emotion of the scene before you actually do it. You know, you've been part of it in the screenwriting, perhaps, or in the preparation of it, in the casting of it, and so there are certain givens that you under-stand, but you can never tell whether something is really holding up until you see the whole thing put together and played in front of an audience. Then you know if it works.

Who were your contemporaries at Oxford?

There was Robert Hardy, who became very famous much later playing Churchill in a television series. And Ken Tynan, who became a distinguished film and theater critic.

There was Sandy Wilson, who wrote *The Boy Friend* and had an enormous success with that. Tynan was the most famous.

Somebody you didn't get on with particularly well.

Not terribly well, no. We were all very conscious—those of us who wanted to become professional actors, or whatever it was, of a professional avenue into the theater. We were very conscious of trying to make an impression. Robert Hardy was perhaps the first of us who became well-known—he went to Stratford very early on after leaving university. We were playing with this dramatic society on tour in France. All the costumes had arrived and the wigs, and I was caught trying on Robert Hardy's wig, which infuriated him. I'd never seen such a "How dare you! This is my bit, and this is my property!" and all that kind of thing. We were behaving like professional actors, I suppose, long before we had any reason to do so. I've never had any formal training either in film or theater. I never went to a drama school, I never went to a film school, and I actually don't regret that.

You were able to try things out at Oxford?

I think that's one of the most important things: you've got to be allowed to make mistakes. When you've made a wrong choice—either in how to play something or how to direct something—the damage cannot be necessarily repaired, but you've got to deal with the mistakes and to be al-

lowed to make them. It's now getting more and more difficult to do so, because of the high cost of mistakes. I mean,
the three most expensive words in movies, I would think,
are: "Let's try this."

Most good directors do use those words.

Absolutely, you have to. It's a risk you have to take. Otherwise you're never going to develop.

**Perhaps Oxford also offered an opportunity to develop other
interests at the same time, whereas kids who go to film
schools tend to become very good technicians but are not
quite as rounded in other ways.**

Well, you know my whole attitude about exclusivity. I'm
not exclusively interested in the cinema. I don't spend my
entire life looking at lost films or films that historically are
important to the cinema. I'm not really terribly interested in
becoming a one-line person, because I've always thought
that the arts inform each other. I'm glad that I had wonderful musical opportunities, because music has been very important to my life and to my work. I'm glad that I've
developed an eye for art and sculpture. It's important to be
able to observe and to use as much as you can. It reinforms
everything else. I enjoy American musicals enormously. And
I still like theater and love opera, so I like the mixture of
things that may or may not influence other things that I've
chosen to do.

*You made your first film that got attention while at Oxford.
But you had not yet made up your mind to be a film director,
or had you?*

No, it became clearer. I made a film in my first year at
Oxford called *Black Legend*. It told the story of a double
murder and subsequent double hanging that took place in
the seventeenth century. The gibbet, which commemorated
these events, had obviously been replaced several times in
Berkshire, on the downs there. That was my first experience
of making a film, based on a real story, and we had enormous pleasure in making it and showing it in various village
halls. But we couldn't afford a sound track. We could only afford performances on twin turntables with music and commentary and effects, and we sort of had to dub the film at
every performance.

*What was it about that particular story that appealed to
you? Was it the macabre quality? It was the story of an
adulterous affair, wasn't it?*

It was the story of an adulterous affair and subsequent
murder of the wife and child that these two people were involved with. We got the details of the trial from the local as-
size book in Newbury and just reconstructed it. We had no
money to speak of. To dress a crowd of two hundred people
we sent a basic costume design to the vicars' wives of various
parishes and told them what we would like the crowds to
look like. It was just after the war, so for blouses and other

costumes we could cut up blackout curtains and things of that sort. We found a way of making it work.

You made the film with Alan Cooke.

Yes. I'd met him on a troopship coming back from the Far East. And I had appeared in—in fact I'd organized—a sort of concert party on board ship and acted and sung in it. When we were auditioning in my first year at Oxford for a review with Sandy Wilson, I remembered that Alan could sing, and we became great friends and eventually lovers. It was a very unsatisfactory relationship really, because he was basically ashamed of it.

But you weren't?

It didn't worry me. I remember playing in a student production of *Epicene,* the Ben Jonson play. We went on tour with it in France, and my tutor, John Bryson, from Balliol was with us. Rather like Pandarus in *Troilus and Cressida,* he wanted to see what happened between Alan and me. After the tour was over, we went off to Lake Como, and my tutor saw us off on the night train, I think hoping that this was going to come to some positive conclusion.

A sort of Maurice Bowra figure.

I suppose so, yes. Certainly he became a mentor. I told him about things in my life which I wouldn't have told anyone else at the time, and he was very happy to be put in that position, I think.

Who wrote the script of **Black Legend***?*

Both Alan and myself, and we both directed it, as well as doing the camera work.

This was to be a pattern in your career. You've always collaborated on scripts. Why did you never write your own scripts?

I've never had the confidence.

Why do you think that is? What has held you back?

I never felt confident in my own talent as a writer. I think I probably could have written. But I've never considered myself very good at dialogue. I can think of all sorts of ideas when I'm preparing a film or collaborating on a script, but I've never had the confidence perhaps to just go ahead and write it.

To what extent do you feel that's been a drawback? Because it does make you very dependent on the writing talents of others. I think in your career your best films have all been based on very good scripts, while those that are less successful are often equally well directed but suffer from writing that isn't quite as good.

Absolutely true. But I think if I'd written them they would have been disastrous. Working with such talents as Alan Bennett has been an eye-opener. And an enormous pleasure, because if you know anything about this business, you know it when you've got a good script in your hands. When you've got a script that doesn't work so well, it's like pulling teeth, and very often we've had to call in other writers.

Black Legend *was your first feature film. What did you learn from that experience cinematically?*

The main thing was rhythm. I think it's very important to think of a film rather like a musical score. You are dealing with an audience, and to hook an audience into the story and to keep their interest alive is a question of pacing and rhythm. I've always liked storytelling, and I think that one of the things that I've learned is how to tell a story visually. There is too much chat in films, and there used to be much more. I admire films which tell a story visually, as much as possible. A lot of it comes down to the editing. Some people know nothing about editing and go to the cutting room with no ideas. But I have a lot of ideas about rhythm and editing, and I'm very good at it and enjoy it hugely. This doesn't mean that I haven't made terrible mistakes, but there are various techniques which you learn over the years. When I was making *A Kind of Loving,* I didn't know the grammar of constructing a scene—didn't know how to tell the story. The cameraman would complain bitterly that I hadn't done my homework.

You also cut **Black Legend** *together with Alan Cooke?*

Oh, yes, I suppose we did. There was a very competitive streak in the way we behaved, because he wanted to become a director professionally and became one, I think, sooner than I did. Our emotional connection wasn't necessarily a good thing either.

While the film was being made?

Before and during, yes. On the whole, I found emotional involvement with people I was working with not a good thing and have avoided it mostly.

You're not an example of a director who always had an affair with the leading lady or leading man.

No, do you know, I never thought that I was going to be excited by working with A, B, or C. The proof of the pudding is that you don't want really anything to do with them. I suppose Alan Bates, who is still a very good friend, is the only actor whom I felt I was in love with, when we were making *A Kind of Loving*. And I've never felt that since.

Did you keep these feelings to yourself?

I don't know to what extent I kept them entirely to myself. I avoided having dinners with the producer, much to his anger, because he wanted to talk shop, and I wanted to talk to my leading man. But nothing ever came of it.

Have you ever discussed this with him?

Oh, yes, because we laugh about things a great deal.

Do you think it sharpened the performance in any way? Did it work in an inspiring manner, or do you think that it made things more difficult?

No, it didn't make things more difficult. I think maybe it sharpened it. It certainly made me pay more attention to directing him, but I was aware that he was also having an affair with the leading lady, June Ritchie, while we were shooting, and in a funny way I encouraged that, because I thought it heightened the performance.

What did you do after Black Legend?

I made another film when I was at Oxford, called *The Starfish.* It was a fantasy about a sea witch, played by my aunt, whom I nearly drowned. It wasn't any good, and we blew it up from 16 millimeter to 35 and got some kind of a release. There was a marvelous character called Mr. Phillips, who ran the distribution. "What do you want to do this for?" he would say in a lovely Jewish accent, "Oh my God, you want to make it a professional film, and it isn't a professional film." I said that we were trying to make it so—"Well, I don't know—oh, God, oh." That went on a lot, but it didn't do any business. I remember sitting in an audience in the cinema with it and someone saying behind me: "Well, someone must have had fun doing that."

How were these student films financed? They can't have been cheap.

Two hundred pounds.

Expensive for the time.

For the time, yes. My family helped and my grandmother. They were very instrumental in all this, providing us with food and shelter for people who were taking part in the film. And we begged, borrowed, or stole all sorts of things. There was a local timber yard which built things for nothing for us. And we got petrol for jeeps and things to get around from generous farmers. It was quite a good preparation for knowing how to get something for nothing as much as you can.

Black Legend was really my best memory of the innocence of filmmaking, when it was all fun and not terribly serious. I remember, for example, when we came to the hanging scene, which was great fun to do, and we had a crowd of about two hundred, I decided that for one of the executions we should hang the camera on the end of a rope and keep it running and then drop it. And of course it broke. As a result of this, we were rather stymied. We had to stop shooting and take the camera up to London to try and get it repaired. It's in the film. But there is something wonderful about responsibility not being so desperate, when you can really act upon the words "Let's try this," I mean, in the most cack-handed, amateur fashion. It was an amateur film—no question.

But it got shown to some important people.

Dylis Powell saw it. She was a wonderfully elegant woman and a distinguished critic for the *Sunday Times* in the days when one still thought of some critics as distinguished. And she headed her review of the film "Brains, Not Money," which I've always remembered and been immensely grateful for, because it did draw attention to us and the film when we were hoping for some sort of recognition and a job out of it. I was rather keen to get to Ealing as an assistant assistant assistant teaboy or whatever—I didn't mind what it was. Alfred Shaughnessy, who was in charge of publicity at the Ealing Studios, came and wrote a very nice appreciation of the film, which Michael Balcon saw, and we were summoned to show the film to all their henchmen at the studio.

So what came out of all this?

Nothing.

A disappointment . . .

Jobs were very, very difficult to come by. It was one of the perennial periods of a slump in British cinema, and I couldn't get arrested.

But it must have boosted your confidence.

It certainly did. They were great days, even though I might have been despairing and saying it was all dreadful, which I normally did, in the hopes that it wouldn't be—a kind of Jewish negative feeling: oy vey! It's terrible, what are we going to do! I don't know when exactly my parents decided that I wasn't a total write-off—for I was a write-off in everything before that. But I think they recognized my talent and, more than that, the quality of not taking no for an answer, of battering down doors.

——

You said earlier that when you were at school you were inspired and excited by the German expressionists. Were you interested in British cinema? Didn't you run a film club at Oxford?

I was part of a film club, but I don't think I ran it. In my time at Oxford I was president of the Experimental Theatre Club, as well as being a member of the Oxford University Dramatic Society. I was more interested, I think, in being an actor in those days. I never envisaged myself with the responsibility of producing and being a front man for films. I never thought that was my talent, although subsequently I'd done quite a lot of work of the producer, even when I've been making professional films. Because presentation and showmanship and all that was just as important to me as the film itself. I've often wondered what it would have been like to have run a theater like the Everyman Cinema in London. I'd quite like to have done that at one time.

Who were the big names in British cinema then?

I suppose Alexander Mackendrick, you know, the Ealing people. There was Basil Dearden, whom I worked with subsequently doing second unit on a television series. I thought he was great because he didn't feel threatened by me, as some of the other directors did, who would rather do everything themselves.

Did filmmakers of your generation rebel against these older directors, in the way young French New Wave directors reacted against the old generation?

I don't think I was really rebellious. I know what I *did* rebel against: the sort of fuddy-duddiness of the Oxford Film Society types who were talking in a very simplistic way of an approach to making films. Of how you've got to have a long shot, and then you've got to have this and that, and I thought there was a freer and more open way of viewing the cinema without particular reference to British film. I wanted to break away from that—and did. I didn't want to learn how to take long shots, I knew how to take long shots. I knew how to operate a 16-millimeter camera.

But you didn't feel the need to react against a British tradition?

There were heavily critical people, like Lindsay Anderson, whom I never really got on with. He had a strong sense of being critical of all things British and was quite a rude man. But we were at opposite ends of the pole. I was never really interested in British cinema per se, even though I went to see British films, and I liked the Ealing tradition of films. The directors who were under that umbrella worked well as a group. I don't think they would ever have operated so successfully independently.

European cinema was written about a great deal in those days—the French New Wave, the Italian neorealists. *Films and Filming* was a popular magazine, and *Sight and Sound* was the British Film Institute journal. But I was conscious of not being welcome in this sort of group. I never felt accepted by *Sight and Sound.* In fact, a friend of mine wrote for it and wanted to do an extended interview with me, and it was stopped.

So this was more Ken Tynan's crowd at Oxford?

Well, it was Penelope Houston who edited it, and I never felt comfortable with any of these people.

Nonetheless, I can imagine people of your age getting tired of blimpish war movies and Kenneth More in his tweed jacket and that kind of thing. There was an anarchic quality to the Ealing comedies, so that was a bit different, but there was also a rather boring, jingoistic mainstream of British cinema.

The Anna Neagle type of film. Herbert Wilcox, her husband, directed them. Those feel-good movies, such as *Spring in Park Lane,* were obviously a reaction to the war. And I came along at a time when Tony Richardson and John Osborne had formed Woodfall Films. They held a tight control over their own products and offered a different feeling. The kind of gritty realistic films that were being made at that time were an important phase, and I tagged on to that.

Did you see films like **Rome, Open City** *at the time and* **Bicycle Thieves?**

Very much so. Vittorio De Sica became a kind of god to me. Another film that influenced me was *Ikiru*—I was very interested in Kurosawa. And Fellini's films. I was less interested in the more intellectual filmmakers—Antonioni or even Bergman, who had a sort of alien quality which I didn't like. I very much like humanistic films.

It sounds as though your rebellion was more formalistic than political, unlike Lindsay Anderson, say.

Yes, they were political, and I never regarded myself as particularly political. Now, of course, one realizes that everything is political, and you can't escape it. But it wasn't something that I was passionate about.

Did the political filmmakers regard you as not quite trustworthy?

They regarded me as an intruder, I think, particularly when I asked Miriam Brickman, who was the casting director at the Royal Court, to come and cast one of my films— indeed, several of my films subsequently. They thought that was a terrible poaching on their preserves, or at least I believe they did. I never felt part of their movement, even though I'm often lumped together with them. I'd nothing to do with Free Cinema, which was something that a whole group of people, including Karel Reisz and Lindsay Anderson, formed as a sort of breakaway group from the more old-fashioned attitudes of British filmmaking. But, you know, I got over all of that and treasured the fact that I made *A Kind of Loving* first, which was in the mode of the kitchen sink. That is when I was discovered by and learned a great deal from the wonderful, wonderful producer Joe Janni, a Milanese who had left Italy and come to settle in England.

Let's go back a bit. After Oxford there were several years of being an actor.

Yes, but I wasn't a very good actor. I wouldn't have cast myself probably if I'd come up in front of me for an audition. I knew I wasn't that good.

What was the range of your acting after Oxford?

Well, I played in weekly repertory theater—I can't even remember all the parts. I was at Colchester Rep, and I was a servant in *Julius Caesar*, I think. I was in various comedies. Then I graduated to three-weekly rep, where you had longer to prepare.

Did you still have an ambition to make it as an actor, or was it preparation for something else?

No, I don't think it was. I don't think I ever thought of myself really as director material. I never thought I had the kind of individuality to strike out and do that kind of thing.

I had, at Oxford, entered a competition of one-act plays, as a director, and did a Thornton Wilder play, which was almost foolproof—*A Happy Journey to Trenton and Camden*—and won the competition. People told me I was a director, and I had an inkling that perhaps my talents could lie there. But because I wanted to be an actor, I never seriously pursued it at that stage.

But you did work as an actor with some quite distinguished directors. You were in Michael Powell's film Oh, Rosalinda!! **Did you learn anything from that, or were they just jobs?**

They were jobs. I got on very well with Michael Powell and admired him. But I don't think I was a student of the Powell-Pressberger films. I remember thinking how vulgar their taste was, particularly in design.

I also worked for the Boulting brothers—particularly Roy Boulting, who was a friend. Roy realized I was interested in being a director, encouraged it, and would explain how something was going to be cut together—the scene I was in—and he would show me the lenses and that kind of thing.

He was interested in the fact that I was a stills photographer, and I earned a little bit of money that way, taking pictures of actors. I would ask them what kind of parts they wanted to get from these photographs. It might be bankers or lawyers or crooks or whatever, and I'd put them in those particular situations. If a woman said she wanted to play gypsy parts or religious parts, I'd put a crucifix on the wall and photograph her in that kind of situation. And charge them a few guineas, process the film under the stairs in a sort of makeshift darkroom—the bath was always filled with prints washing.

Making stills is a very different way of photographing from shooting a film. How did it help you develop as a filmmaker?

I think when you're about to preserve a particular moment, it teaches you to wait for that moment and hopefully press the button at the right time. I've always been an enormous admirer of Cartier-Bresson for that reason, because he always seems to judge how to catch the right instant of a particular human moment. I became much more knowledgeable about stills and the kind of tricks of the trade, but all those kinds of things were self-taught and important to learn.

Your love of Cartier-Bresson is another illustration of being drawn to a particular kind of humor, which is one area where I think you were different from the more political directors of your generation. They might have considered your humanism to be bourgeois.

Oh, yes, I'm sure they all thought I was bourgeois, which I probably was and am. But I wasn't going to ask for forgiveness for what I believed interesting and valid. Humanistic cinema was something I became very attached to as a member of the audience, and perish the thought of a more intellectual approach.

I don't know if it's so much intellectual. I think Anderson and perhaps some of the writers who were "angry young men" had more than artistic aims. They wanted to change the world or change society, which was perhaps never your main concern.

No, it wasn't my main concern, but it was my concern, I think, to shake it up to a certain extent and to deal with topics that were not the run-of-the-mill. I've always hated run-of-the-mill. That is why, years later, I came to make my most personal film perhaps—*Sunday Bloody Sunday*—which unashamedly looked at human relationships that weren't the norm. It was my first attempt to do something autobiographical, and I did so without blinking and got pleasantly rewarded for it.

You are known as a very good director of actors. Did your own acting experience have a lot to do with that?

I became attuned to the sensitivity of actors, and I think that's what made me good with actors, because I understood the process a little bit.

Was there a point that you felt you really didn't have what it took to be an actor? Did you consciously want to do something else? Or did you naturally slide into a different career?

Well, I think I knew my future wasn't on the end of a string being occasionally pulled like some puppet. I wanted something that would be all-enveloping and use every quality that I knew a director had a chance to use. And I made these two films as a student at Oxford, and I started to direct a little bit in the theater, like the one-act competition which I won. It was a question of realizing that I had that talent, and I didn't automatically think I did.

Being a director needs a lot of self-confidence, and I just didn't know that I had that at that point. It took me some time to plunge in.

BREAKING IN

From 1956 to 1961, John Schlesinger worked for the BBC, directing short documentary films for the *Monitor* and *Tonight* programs. These included profiles of Georges Simenon and Benjamin Britten. One of his shorts, *The Innocent Eye,* won a diploma at the Edinburgh Festival. His own favorite work of this period was *Italian Opera* (1960), which caught the eye of Joseph Janni, the producer of his first feature film, *A Kind of Loving* (1962). He also made a documentary about four young painters, entitled *A Private View* (1960), and *The Class,* about drama students.

As a freelance filmmaker, John worked on a series on World War II generals for CBS television and did second-unit direction for the TV series *The Four Just Men* (1959), starring Jack Hawkins and Vittorio De Sica. He also shot a publicity film for *The Guns of Navarone* (1961), directed by J. Lee Thompson.

The film that launched him in the cinema was *Terminus* (1961), a thirty-minute documentary about twenty-four hours at Waterloo Station, commissioned by British Transport Films. It got wide distribution and won the Golden Lion award at the Venice Film Festival and a British Academy Film Award.

You spoke earlier about learning the grammar of film-making. But you began your professional career making documentaries. Your first big success was Terminus, *a documentary about Waterloo Station. The grammar of a documentary film must be rather different from that of feature films. How did you learn your craft in those years?*

By experimentation, by cutting film in a certain way, by thinking of it in a certain kind of structure. And then finding myself all at sea in feature films when I had to actually do a scene which had a beginning, a middle, and an end, and one was dealing with actors as well as camera angles.

The main thing, though, is observation. That's one of the pleasures of being a director. Observation is part of my professional life, obviously, but it also gives me great pleasure. I remember working with an actor, and after rehearsals we used to sit in the lobby of a large hotel in Piccadilly and put professions and names to everyone who came in and imagine their relationships and come up with some extraordinary fantasy of their lives. It was a great game, but it can also be quite pertinent, because you study faces and you imagine that the turn of the mouth or whatever tells you something about those people. So I used that a lot in my documentary stuff for the BBC particularly and very much also in *Terminus*. I spent several weeks hanging round Waterloo Station. *Terminus* is full of observed things that I've staged or had to try and catch. The sound was very often put on afterward, because I made it long before cameras were light enough to record at the same time. Videotape does that now.

Purists would probably disapprove of staging scenes in documentary filmmaking. Would you say that staging a scene in a documentary is different from doing it in a feature film?

Terminus was a film about twenty-four hours in the life of a railway station, and a lot of it *had* to be staged. But you're not dealing with big scenes in documentaries. The biggest scene we staged was of a lost boy who was, in fact, a distant relative. We had to do tests to find out who was the most sensitive boy, who would break down away from his mother, and we found that he was what we wanted.

Didn't you do something to deliberately upset him?

You've got to use whatever means you can to get the reaction you want. There's a famous story about Carol Reed making *The Fallen Idol*. To make a child cry, he gave him a toy to play with and then took it away and broke it in front of the child (having prepared a new one, without the child knowing it). I did the same sort of thing in *Terminus*. We got the boy to cry by giving him a bar of chocolate and then taking it away from him.

How did you get to make **Terminus***?*

Edgar Anstey, who was then running British Transport Films, had seen a whole spool of my work for television and said: "You must come and do a film for us. What would you like to do?" And I said I'd like to do a film about Brighton, because I enjoyed visiting Brighton very much. It had a mixture of sleaze and a sort of glamour of its own: the Regency crescents and that extraordinary palace—Brighton Pavilion. And he told me to go ahead and research it, so I wrote a treatment, illustrated by lots of photographs of Brighton, and that sort of thing. But he passed on it, saying it wasn't "central enough to the kind of films that we want to make. Think again." So I said: "Well, twenty-four hours in the life of a railway station." I had a fortnight to do it in and a great deal of film at the end of it, and it took us quite a long time to find the structure, because very often in a documentary you find the structure in the cutting room more than you do beforehand.

How scripted was it?

It was scripted to a point. I knew that I wanted the boat trains taking off. I didn't know I wanted somebody with a braying laugh—that was something that happened. I did want to do a sequence about lost property and a woman trying to find a specific umbrella. I wanted to do something about death and incarceration of people. This was all stuff that I'd seen, but I knew it would have to be reconstructed.

The way they dealt with the lost child was something that I'd seen but had to re-create. Also, the night sequence with the woman who was using eye makeup to paint her lips. That was something that we actually saw, so we didn't have to re-create it. We followed a real person doing it. It was a very big cutting-room job, and it had enormous success at the London Film Festival. It was shown on the opening night as the shorter film with a Jacques Demy film, I think.

Was it well received by the critics?

I remember a very bitchy notice from Ken Tynan. But you know, you have to—it's difficult to say this, because it's not often that one can stick to this—try not to be affected by notices. Preferably, by not reading them.

But you enjoy reading good notices.

Yes, sure. I like to read that something's been appreciated and that it's got through to an audience. And *Terminus* got so many awards that it was gratifying. It also got a release. It was the first time that I'd made something that was going to be shown on a circuit at the cinema, so I was thrilled. It would be silly to say I don't take any notice of this kind of thing, that I don't read the notices. But I quite often don't.

But is it the bad notices that usually stick in your mind?

Yes, always the bad notices.

Some of what you say about observing scenes that you sub-sequently re-create reminds me of **Midnight Cowboy.** *That sequence with the woman drug addict and her child in the cafeteria, playing with the toy mouse . . .*

Well, I actually saw these things, in fact, in Los Angeles on Hollywood Boulevard. There were places there to hang out and watch the drug life of the city. I saw that very incident and thought it was something that he would remember seeing, the cowboy, and being frightened by it—it certainly scared me.

When you worked on **Terminus,** *or later on, in feature films, when you do your research, do you hang around possible locations making notes of these things?*

Yes, yes, I did. And do. Because, you know, sometimes you see things which you don't expect to see in certain contexts. I mean, the prisoners going off in chains, in *Terminus,* was something that never occurred to me I'd see in a station. I don't know why, because it obviously happens. And I love sequences on trains. I will always remember a Hitchcock film of the 1930s—*The Lady Vanishes*—with Michael Redgrave and Margaret Lockwood and a whole host of wonderful actors. It had a really spooky atmosphere. And the way Hitchcock visualized ideas, like the message written on a piece of paper that stuck to the window for a moment, which announced that someone was in danger—marvelous storytelling and a great deal of tension. It was one of my very favorite films at the time, and I was haunted by the image of the woman bandaged up entirely with just a breathing space for the nose. I was haunted by that film.

Was this related to any memory you might have had?

I took a job once, when I was in a military hospital just before I left the army, folding dressings. And other things took me near the operating theater. I liked seeing people come out with some tube stuck in their mouth. It looked dramatic. *A Kind of Loving* had various scenes in hospitals, too. When we were doing research for the film, we always seemed to come at the moment when an amputation had just taken place, and someone was rushing out of the operating theater with a bucket with what looked like the shape of a limb covered in some green cloth. I suppose anything which has drama attached to it fascinates me. That's why I'm also interested in prisons, because there is a sort of pressurized feeling about a prison.

What is the drama of these places—prisons and trains and buses? Is it because people are locked in with strangers and captive to that situation?

I suppose it's partly that. It's all part of the pressure that the individual is under in his or her life. I remember when we were going to do *The Falcon and the Snowman*, and we were looking at locations in Mexico and saw the type of thing they had in death cells. There was this empty cell— the man was out on exercise, I think. Everything was in order, the bunk was made and everything, and there on the table was a jar of Vaseline prominently displayed, which I imagined had sexual overtones.

I can't think why else it would be there.

No—exactly.

You never did a documentary in a prison?

No. I had scenes in prisons and coming out of prisons. *Billy Liar* has a sequence in a prison. And in *Terminus* there's a group of prisoners chained together. I saw that happening but wasn't allowed to photograph them, so we had to do it with a load of extras. Prisons, like hospitals, are dramatic places. I once did a lecture in a prison. And I asked some people to come with me. We were joined by a—"starlet" I think would be the right description—from one of the studios. She came in the most provocative outfit, with feather boas, and I thought this was embarrassing. I asked her why she was dressed up like that: "Are you trying to give them a sexual thrill?" She said: "Well, of course, dear. That's what they want, don't they?" I thought no, that's unfair. But it went very well, and there was a lot of whistling. They seemed to enjoy this scantily dressed Rank star.

There is a whole genre of prison movies. You've never thought of making one?

Yes, I did. There was recently a novel about a prison. I think they made the film—I don't know what it was like— in which one of the themes was the AIDS ward of the prison hospital. They planned to attack it and get rid of the people inside. It was a very nasty story about rebellion in prison. When I started to think about it, I thought I would be doing this for the wrong reason, for sensational reasons. I'm glad I didn't do it. But it's something that interests me. I remember a party being given in a disused prison in L.A. by, what is his name, the famous writer with a very high-pitched voice? Truman Capote?

Yes, he **would** *have a party in a prison.*

I think the food was laid out in the death cell, which was most intriguing.

Wasn't one of your first documentary films about cheese?

I got a job being a researcher for a documentary about British cheese called *Mousetrap Is Out,* with John Arlott.

How did that come about?

It was a sponsored film, and I just got the chance to go out and research it and traveled round the country visiting various production centers of different cheeses—Cheddar, Stilton, Wensleydale in Yorkshire, and all that kind of thing. I learned quite a lot of things about cheese making, and I found it absolutely fascinating, but I was able to, in the research, stress the nature of the characters who dealt with the sort of Jaguar of cheese making, which was Stilton, and also of the testers and makers of other kinds of cheeses. They interested me as people.

Did this make you want to do more documentaries?

It gave me some experience. I then asked to be made assistant on the film and found that I wasn't bad at producing sandwiches for lunch for the crew in the middle of nowhere, and I enjoyed the whole process.

Wasn't there a film about General Montgomery, too?

That was when I got a job working for an American company, CBS, directing some interviews with famous generals and things for a series about Winston Churchill. We did an interview with Earl Mountbatten, when the continuity girl whispered to me, "There's a hair out of place," and he caught a little bit of that: "What's wrong, what's wrong?" "Er, there's just a hair that's catching the light." "Well, pull it out, for God's sake!"

Montgomery hated the Americans and didn't quite understand what was required of him, because we usually wanted a mute shot of him walking somewhere, so we could put a bit of commentary over it. And he kept talking. We said, "Come out of the house now" as the cameraman was getting very fussy about the light, and he'd say, "No good, no good," so we'd say, "Sorry, sir, would you mind going back?" "What, what, what's wrong?" So we said, "Well, I'm afraid the light's gone." "Oh, has it, all right. Can't do this too many times, you know. Can't do it too many times." He always repeated himself. Couldn't pronounce his "r"s, either. He said to me when he arrived: "Who are you?" So I said: "Well, I'm the director, sir." "Oh, you're the commander in chief of the whole operation, are you, commander in chief of the whole operation. Well, I won't have you in the house. Going to do it in the map room, in the map room."

The map room was a place with gelatin glistening all over the wall, which reflected light terribly, but that's where he wanted to be, and if suddenly we had to stop because of an airplane, I'd say: "Sorry, we've got to cut." "What?" "We've got to cut." "Oh, why's that?" So I said, "Because there's an airplane, and it won't cut together." "Why won't it cut together?" "I can't explain, sir, but it's a technical thing." "Yes, probably an American one!"

Generals are a little like opera stars.

Oh, absolutely. Opera stars in their own way. But there were gentler ones, too. Alanbrooke was a great ornithologist. We did him in the War Office, and he didn't want to be shown coming in and having difficulty with the stairs, so we had to get him in through the back way and take him in the lift.

You didn't do any of the Americans?

No, no, we didn't. We did the great cake maker who did celebratory cakes for Churchill. She was French and got rather muddled up.

How did you get into BBC Television?

I got the chance to make the film that you were in as a child, called *Sunday in the Park*, which was a very facetious, knowing film. I didn't like it much.

But it was shown?

Yes, it was shown. And it was my ticket into the BBC. I first joined a nightly magazine program as a freelance and made short one-minute or five-minute films—snippets—to go in the program. I did this once a month and earned a pittance, but at least it was something, a beginning. I didn't get on with the producer. I hated being called "boy." "It's not funny, boy," he used to say. We would never agree—his sense of humor was so totally unlike mine. I did about a dozen films for them. It was like a factory. Someone else looked after the choice of music and the dubbing, and I didn't want to do that. I wanted to make my own stamp, and they got very fed up with me, and then I got the push. Thank God, Huw Wheldon, another television producer, was waiting in the wings to grab me for an arts-magazine program called *Monitor*.

What was it like?

Huw Wheldon was a very good producer and understood people's individual likes and dislikes and problems and strengths and weaknesses. He was terrific, and I enjoyed working with him enormously. I did all sorts of interesting subjects. The opening film of the program, when it first came on, was a film I made about the circus—an impressionistic film of the years the Russians first performed in an international circus, and it was a rather good piece. There wasn't a word spoken on it, no commentary, and it had no story line; it was just an impression. It did rather well. And I went on to do films about the Brussels Exhibition of that period, and American artists living in Paris, and Brighton Pier.

It was very unusual in those days to have documentaries without commentary. Did you find the common style of blanket narration boring?

That was the way television documentaries were often made, so I was quite used to it. I did a film about Georges Simenon, the thriller writer, which was a lot of interview. But his routine was very interesting. He used to get up early in the morning, go down to his office, and prepare the routine of his pipes, which he smoked endlessly, and the pencils had to be arranged in the same way and sharpened beforehand. And the blank sheets of paper had to be placed before he started writing. The routine was interesting, and we could illustrate it visually. But otherwise it was mostly chat and discussion and questions and answers, which Huw Wheldon himself did.

To what extent did you feel that trying out new things ran up against trusted and tried formulas?

Oh, yes, that happened. At *Monitor*, we'd sit down and discuss what we'd do this month, and I said there was a scratch company coming to Theatre Royal, Drury Lane—an opera company from Italy. I wanted to follow them at rehearsal, backstage, dressing rooms, having spaghetti afterward, or whatever, and the Ealing Studios, which was the center of film operations for the BBC then, said that this was ludicrous, because the cameraman I wanted to work with said that there wasn't sufficient light. But there was a renegade cameraman who said they were all talking nonsense, because he could use very fast stock and get an exposure, so we should do it without listening to rules and regulations. And we did. When they saw the rushes, they rather poohpoohed them, because they weren't all perfectly exposed or anything like that, but I managed to get backstage shots of this marvelously scratch opera company. It was rough-and-ready stuff, but this man, a cameraman by the name of Charles De Jaeger, was just my sort of person. He infuriated the front office at Ealing Studios.

I've always rather enjoyed that—breaking the rules. I think rules of all sorts are made to be broken, and I flourished under those circumstances.

You left Monitor. *Was it the run-ins with the rule makers that made you leave?*

No, no. I just needed another set of experiences. I needed to work as second-unit director on *The Four Just Men*, which is when I first met Basil Dearden, who was one of the directors of the series. That kind of experience of having to fit into someone else's work was fine, I enjoyed doing it. Second unit and commercials. I bummed around, learning whatever I could, wherever I could, and it was great stuff.

As you hadn't made a feature film yet, were you chomping at the bit by then? Did you find that you'd reached the limits of documentary filming?

Well, I certainly wanted to tell stories, yes. I can't say what would have happened if I hadn't got the chance to make *A Kind of Loving*. Would I have continued? Probably. You know, you have to have an incredible amount of patience to deal with the time element, because there is an order of events when you make a film. You could be waiting for ages for the money or for the star—if one's going with stars—to be available, and now more than ever I think the studios want a name that will in some way guarantee the movie. But luckily Joe Janni, my first producer, took the plunge, and I was allowed to make the movie.

Was it the film about the Italian opera troupe that caught his attention?

Yes, that and a film I did about the Central School of Drama, which was at the Swiss Cottage Embassy Theatre, where I'd gone to as a child. I thought I'd pick four students, who were in their final year, and follow them around and watch them and then follow them around when they were trying to get a job in the profession. I thought that would be an interesting film. And it would have been, but I totally changed my tack when I came across a marvelous teacher, an actor called Harold Laing, who had a very interesting class. I decided just to focus on that. It was called *The Class* and took place in this one room. We hardly ever left it, except to look out of the window or into the corridor. It was a very successful piece, which also caught Joe Janni's eye, and they showed it at the National Film Theatre one Saturday morning. I asked Janni to come because I think he'd not made up his mind who was going to direct *A Kind of Loving*. I think he felt that he wanted a fresh eye, and I begged him to let me have a go at it.

You begged him to let you direct the film?

Yes, I did, because he had said: "I'm interested in discovering you." So I said: "Be my guest, please do." I went for an interview with him, and he asked me what I wanted to do, and whether I'd make commercials. I had already done commercials and did a few for him. Then he said: "I'd like to take the risk of getting you to do your first film" and asked me to do a test of Tom Courtenay for *Billy Liar*—the test was as much for me as it was for Tom. Joe wanted opinions to reinforce his and showed the tape around to say: "Do you think I can trust this man?" Luckily, one of the people he asked was Roy Boulting, who was in a sense a champion of mine. He also asked the cameraman: "Does he know what he's doing?" And the cameraman said, fortunately: "Yes, I think he does."

≡

A *Kind of Loving* (1962), starring Alan Bates and June Ritchie, was John Schlesinger's first feature film. It was adapted from Stan Barstow's novel by Keith Waterhouse and Willis Hall. *A Kind of Loving* won the Golden Bear award at the Berlin International Film Festival.

John's second film, *Billy Liar* (1963), was adapted from the stage by Keith Waterhouse and Willis Hall. It starred Tom Courtenay and helped launch the career of Julie Christie.

Darling (1965), written by Frederic Raphael, won an Academy Award for best screenplay. John was nominated for best director, and Julie Christie won the Oscar for best actress. *Darling* also won the New York Film Critics Circle awards for best picture and best director. The other leading actors in *Darling* were Dirk Bogarde and Laurence Harvey.

Julie Christie starred again in *Far from the Madding*

Crowd (1967), adapted by Frederic Raphael from Thomas Hardy's novel. Alan Bates, Terence Stamp, and Peter Finch played the other main roles.

John directed three theater productions for the Royal Shakespeare Company: *No, Why* (1964), *Timon of Athens* (1965), and *Days in the Trees* (1966). In 1967, John directed *Days in the Trees,* with Peggy Ashcroft, for television.

What attracted you to A Kind of Loving? *Was it simply that you were desperate to do a feature film, and this was your chance, or was there something about the story which particularly appealed to you?*

I think it was a mixture of things. It was partly because the story concerned a compromise relationship, the question whether or not you stick it out through thick and a lot of thin—with the mother-in-law forever living there, beautifully but monstrously played by Thora Hird. I thought it was a wonderful human story. And Alan Bates was glorious in it, as was June Ritchie, who had never been seen, really.

And hasn't been seen much since.

Not a great deal. It wasn't that she wasn't good, but she opted for a family life. Children and so forth.

Can you describe what it felt like when you went onto the set for the first time?

It was in a suburb of Manchester. Alan Bates and I were sharing a car. We were driven to the location, and suddenly I saw all these trucks and lights and things and the assembled unit getting ready for my arrival and waiting for me to tell them what I wanted. And I was about to say to the driver: "Turn round, let's go back to the hotel." Although I'd worked out what I wanted to shoot, confronting the crew for the first time is an alarming business when you've never done it before. And I had a rather bad-tempered director of photography who complained that I didn't know what I was doing—which I didn't. Thank God I had a marvelous camera operator, Johnny Morris, who stuck with me and suggested things which made a lot of sense and which I wouldn't have known about. I had him on several films subsequently. He was a wonderful help. I would have to say about first films that you want experienced people around you who know what they're doing.

So how far had you worked it out? To what extent did you have it in your head or on paper how you were going to shoot a scene?

I don't think I knew how to break a sequence. I could work out camera angles according to a plan. And people would make suggestions. One problem in *A Kind of Loving* is that we lost the light. We were shooting in November, and we had a scene to do on the hills outside the town and we lost the light completely. So we had to light it and try and make it cut in. We weren't able to add it to another day's schedule, it just wasn't practical. So, with a very heavy heart I shot it that way and hated doing it. I thought it wouldn't look real—and it doesn't—but I don't know whether other people noticed or not. Now I'm much more easy about breaking rules—shooting under protest, as they call it.

Except then you didn't really know what the rules were?
No.

Could that also be a help, in the sense that it might make you less inhibited?

Yes, but you know it's very terrifying, the reality of schedules. Because of the money and the fact that you're under pressure from the producer—"Come on, you must be quicker."

Was there a lot of pressure from Joe Janni?

It was tough, but I was devoted to Joe, who had a great sense of humor. Like so many Italians, he drove like a madman. When we shot *A Kind of Loving,* he was convinced I was directing the film too slowly, and he was in the sound truck listening to the tapes and said: "I'm sure this should be faster." And I said, "No, Joe, it's the right speed. If it's faster it will look as if they've learned their lines too pat. I want it less pat." He accepted this, and I was right—I'm not always right.

The interiors were shot at Shepperton Studios?

Yes. We shot interiors in the studio and even had back projection—an anathema to me then—outside the windows, so we could see what was going on in the garden or the grounds of the house or school or whatever. I thought we saw it too well. It should have been out of focus to give us a sense of distance.

Do things like that make you wince when you see the film now?

I haven't seen it for a long time. But you know, a film is made at a certain time in your life, and I prefer the warts-and-all attitude to "Let's do it again." I mean, it's a good film. For a first film it's amazing and was very well received.

The subject of compromises people make in their relationships is something that comes back in other films as well. Does this preoccupation reflect things in your own life?

It does preoccupy me, I suppose. Nothing is as ideal as it seems. It needs a lot of work and a great deal of compromise for a relationship to survive. I really believe that, and it's been so in my own life. I've been with my present partner, Michael Childers, for thirty-four years. We spend quite a lot of time apart, which probably is very good for us. It's something that I've learnt to accept. The words of Cole Porter— "I'm always true to you, darling, in my fashion, I'm always true to you, darling, in my way"—are very true.

I think it's even one of the lines in Sunday Bloody Sunday— *"I'd rather had half a loaf than no bread at all." The doctor says this, doesn't he?*

Yes, I think that's right. Glenda Jackson plays the divorced woman who is having an affair simultaneously with the doctor and with this young inventor/sculptor, who's very much a product of the time. We were making the film in 1971, so it's some years ago, and it was a film that was completely original. It wasn't based on a book or a short story or anything like that. It was part of my own experience.

But the woman was the one who wouldn't accept a compromise relationship, whereas the doctor says that he would accept it. So the doctor is more a reflection of your own sensibility than the woman in that story?

Possibly. Yes, yes it is.

Whereas A Kind of Loving *is a little bit different, I suppose, in that it's harder to feel that the main character has made the right choice.*

I think it's of its period. People now aren't prepared to work at a relationship or to accept things easily that may not be obvious. The doctor in *Sunday Bloody Sunday* was based on myself. The story goes back to the 1960s when I was directing my first play for the Royal Shakespeare Company, which was a one-act play by John Whiting. I had a very intense affair with one of the actors—a man who was bisexual. We had a lot of fun and liked each other enormously, but I was more smitten than he was, and something told me that this might be something that I shouldn't pursue—I don't know what—but I did anyway. I used to go to almost every performance, go round with notes, and they were quite unused to directors doing this kind of thing. The cast used to say: "You are incredible, you keep coming round to see us. It's wonderful. We've never had a director like that." Little did they really tumble to the reason.

How close was this story to **Sunday Bloody Sunday?** *Was there also a woman in his life?*

Yes, there was. She had a part in *Darling*.

Was John Whiting then still seeing your youngest sister, Susan? That relationship also involved a lot of compromises.

Yes, it did. My sister was deeply in love with John Whiting, but he was already married and wouldn't divorce. And this resulted in quite a lot of drama in her life and in his life. My father, who was a very humane man, knew that he wasn't making Susan happy and went and confronted John Whiting. He said: "Either make an honest woman of her or end the whole thing"—which is what he did. But his wife, whom he wouldn't divorce, allowed Susan to nurse John when he had a virulent form of cancer, with herself in attendance. He wasn't cut out of her life.

Did you know Whiting before, or did you know him through her?

Through her, probably. He knew I wanted to have some experience in theater and had the ear of Peter Hall, who asked me to do this one-act play. And as a result of that I was invited to go to Stratford to do *Timon of Athens* with Paul Scofield, which was a frightening job because I'd never done Shakespeare before and didn't really know it. I'd read it at Oxford, studied it, and I'd acted in several Shakespeare plays, but I didn't know anything about poetry speaking and dealing with the text. It wasn't my bag at all.

To get back to the theme of A Kind of Loving *and* Sunday Bloody Sunday, *it's not the job of a film director to be a critic, but how aware were you of a common theme in your work? Is it something that starts off being instinctive and you then become conscious of as these things are pointed out to you, or did you already know at the time of* A Kind of Loving *what your main themes were?*

No, I don't think it was anything as structured as that. I know by the way you questioned me that you would like an answer that has a structure to it, that impinges on the rest of my life. But, you know, I work off-the-cuff very much. It's taken me quite a long time to realize what the connecting tissue is in my work. But they are all connected. The themes that I've chosen to do are very often about the outsider or compromise. Take *Far from the Madding Crowd*. Thomas Hardy was always writing, or very often writing, about fate or providential attack on an individual who's trying to keep upright in the storm. Fate is constantly striking the individual down, but he has to get up and resist, which in a way is about compromise. That's why the theme of *Far from the*

John Schlesinger in the park with his nanny.

Playing a jester in an Oxford University production of *The Tempest*.

ABOVE: With Alan Bates, filming *A Kind of Loving*. COURTESY OF VIC FILMS
LEFT: On the set of *Billy Liar*. COURTESY OF VIC FILMS

With Julie Christie, filming *Darling*.

Clowning on location for *Billy Liar*.

On location in Texas
for *Midnight Cowboy*.

Directing *Sunday Bloody Sunday*, with Glenda Jackson in the background.

With Joseph Janni, producer of *Sunday Bloody Sunday*.

Directing William Atherton and Karen Black on location for *The Day of the Locust*.

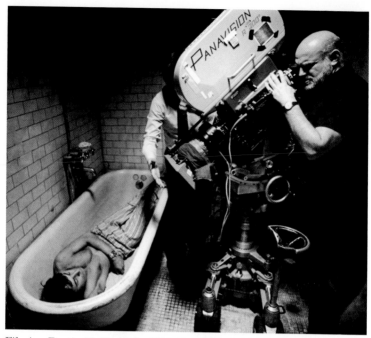

Filming Dustin Hoffman for *Marathon Man*. COURTESY OF PARAMOUNT PICTURES

With Laurence
Olivier on location
in New York for
Marathon Man.
COURTESY OF
PARAMOUNT PICTURES

ABOVE: With
Richard Gere and
Vanessa Redgrave
on the set of *Yanks*.
COURTESY OF CIP
FILMPRODUKTION
GMBH

LEFT: On the set
of *Honky Tonk
Freeway*.
COURTESY OF
MICHAEL CHILDERS

With Coral Browne playing herself in *An Englishman Abroad*.

John Schlesinger on the set of *Billy Liar*.

Madding Crowd appealed to me. Or *Darling,* where the main character, played by Julie Christie, thinks that something better is always around the next corner and therefore won't commit to anything, with disastrous results, of course. They've all got something in common. The opera I'm doing at the moment—*Peter Grimes*—is about paranoia and distrust and prejudice and a man who realizes that he has to destroy himself. All the themes I have chosen are not quite as melodramatic, perhaps, as that.

Yes, I didn't ask you this expecting you to provide a structure. I asked for the opposite reason. It might be a bad thing to be too aware of common themes, to try to explain yourself too much. Perhaps one should forget about it.

I think that one should try and forget about it, but often it's the truth. I mean, it *is* the common link between the subjects I've chosen to do, which are quite often in a sense pessimistic, but I hope not totally so, because I think that hope is something that's very important to pursue.

The script for A Kind of Loving *was written by Keith Waterhouse and Willis Hall. What was it like to work with them?*

Perfectly practical. But I probably didn't work with them enough. I didn't know quite what to do. So I was a good listener to what they were proposing. There were things that didn't work and we needed to have another go at later on. The whole process was foreign to me. The main thing I learned from making *A Kind of Loving* was the basic way of breaking up a scene, therefore editing a scene—the question, for example, whether, as became fashionable, one wanted to do everything in wider shots and not go in for emphasis to close-ups; I've always liked close-ups; I think a lot can be told of what a character is going through by the closeness of the camera. I don't mean just showing a mouth, because that draws attention to itself, though sometimes you have to do it. *A Kind of Loving* was a classically shot film, in which there was no need for a lot of tricky cutting—that came later. By the time I did *Midnight Cowboy*, I'd really started to throw caution to the wind.

***You didn't feel confident enough to break the rules in* A Kind of Loving?**

You can break rules—and should—but there's a way of telling a story so that it looks effortless, and you have to follow rules about direction of film: where people are looking and how you deal with the left-to-right, right-to-left question, so it doesn't jar or jump. Of course, the French cinema of the fifties and sixties did break rules a lot of times.

But that wasn't so common in British films?

No. There was quite a lot of, you know, "You do realize . . . ?" and that kind of thing from the person doing continuity. There's a scene when Alan Bates, having walked out on his mother-in-law and his wife, because they're behaving impossibly, got very drunk and is sick in the living room. I really liked doing this scene, despite a great deal of protest from the crew.

Why?

They thought I was ruining the beautiful emotion of the film. The continuity girl had a lot to say about it: "Why does he have to be sick? Can't he go offstage and be sick?" I said, "We're not doing a Greek play, you know, where things are considered valid in reported speech." It's a dramatic and appalling moment, and the mother's reaction is very funny, which encouraged me to get a prop guy to mix up an extra lot of Sandwich Spread so I could dollop it over the sofa.

The crew's reaction is surprising, because the whole point of kitchen-sink drama was that life was not beautiful—it had to be gritty.

Yes, but they meant that the sensitive spirit of the film was being upset. I've often faced this criticism—that if your leading man, let's say, does something that's unsympathetic, you're going to lose sympathy for him. People said that the end of *Midnight Cowboy* wouldn't work because Joe Buck beats up this old man who picks him up. The fact that he beats him up and knocks his teeth out is not very attractive and could be read as unsympathetic. But I think what he does is totally human, understandable, and necessary for the film. We tried it without that scene, and it was very weak. So we went back to the idea of including it all, but some people were very worried about this whole question of, in inverted commas, "sympathy."

Who is "people"?

Not the producer but the front office, so to speak. But I like things that aren't normal, in a sense that you're taking a risk of losing sympathy. I think that the total picture of a character sometimes has very negative elements but that you need to use it for the audience to understand.

How close was Vic, the Alan Bates character in A Kind of Loving, *to Billy Liar or indeed Joe Buck in* Midnight Cowboy?

Not at all. Not really. He wasn't the same sort of character. He wanted to do the right thing, which is something that's never considered these days.

Did you feel more akin to the Billy Liar character?

Yes, in a way I think I did.

Billy Liar *(1963) begins with a tracking shot going past a lot of suburban houses with Godfrey Winn on the radio.*

The opening shot is all about the similarity of dwellings. Remember, it's allied with a sound track of a popular radio show playing the music that housewives had written in for. It was a very famous program called *Housewives' Choice*, presented by Godfrey Winn, a well-known popular journalist. He couldn't pronounce his "r"s, so I tried to put as many "r"s into the announcement as possible. Not to show him up, but because it was a character point. You know: "This is Betty Bwadley who's wequested whatever"—some terrible, overused piece of light classical music. When the film was first shown, the audience applauded this opening sequence. I was very pleased that I'd hit the spot. It's about feeling free enough to use anything and any way of telling the story, as unliterally as possible. I think that's very important to learn to do—and I did.

How did Billy Liar *come your way?*

I was asked to do it quite a long time before I encountered Joe Janni, when I was directing second unit on *The Four Just Men*. This was when I was still bumming around as a freelance. When you do second unit, you're topping and tailing scenes, which might later be shot in a studio. It was quite interesting to do because I was directing De Sica, who was an idol of mine. I absolutely worshipped the ground that he walked on. This was after *Bicycle Thieves* and his other famous films. De Sica was a great gambler. I remember taking him to dinner at a restaurant which also was an early gambling club, and I think he was doing these television films in order to pay off his debts. An extraordinary man.

How did this tie in with Billy Liar?

The producer of *The Four Just Men* had this book, gave it to me to read, and asked me whether I wanted to do it. Of course, I wanted to very much, but nobody would back me as I had no experience. So I had to wait until Joe Janni bought the rights and asked me to do it, warning me to make up my mind quickly, because Karel Reisz was considering it very carefully. And I thought, No, not on your nelly! I'm going to do it. So I did.

Were you still terrified?

Not as much as with the first film, but even today it's quite nerve-racking to start a new project. It's said that very often the first week of shooting is all for the cutting-room floor, and sometimes in those days you could afford to do that. The kind of thing that Woody Allen does. But now you can't do that—well, Woody Allen may, but us mortals have to toe the line a bit more for financial reasons.

Your films are not conceived in the cutting room in the way they are with some filmmakers?

I think you can do an awful lot in the cutting room, and I enjoy that part of the procedure. You often shoot much more than you need to tell the story. You've got to assume that the audience is quicker than they're given credit for— because they are. That's one of the things I learned by doing commercials. That you can tell a story very quickly.

But I think it's very good to know what you're going to do, even though I don't personally want to be slavish to a blueprint. Because sometimes you've really got to think of something in a different way. I happen to have my last script, no, not quite—*Eye for an Eye*—and you'll notice there's hardly a white page in there.

It's more worked out than A Kind of Loving?

Much more, because I knew the grammar, I knew what I wanted to do, where everybody was going to be, how we were going to edit it.

Billy Liar *looks quite different from* A Kind of Loving.

Billy Liar wasn't a linear story because it was interrupted all the time by fantasies, which is why I chose to do it in CinemaScope, so that the screen was a bigger space. One had a margin to work in. And great fun it was.

What was it like to work with Tom Courtenay? Was there ever any question of Alan Bates playing that part?

No. Albert Finney had done the stage version, and Courtenay took over. Tom didn't have the roguish element of Finney, but I thought he gave a very moving and well-developed performance.

Courtenay may be better at playing the weakness of a man who can't really cope with life.

I didn't see it as weakness. Just because he couldn't face leaving home, I don't think that's necessarily weak. His decision to stay and live through his fantasy life was just as valid.

That's very interesting. Would you describe Billy Liar's life as another variation of playing with the cards you've got and compromising?

Well, I wouldn't have called it compromising. Billy is a character who could not bear a kind of set existence—he had to live through his imagination. And his imagination let him down only because he didn't dare—when the opportunity came to throw everything over, he didn't dare to do it. So he preferred to march home with his fantasy. That's why I'm very keen on the end, when you see him marching up the street with his army, his fantasy army. And then, you know, he's alone.

A shot that is echoed in the last scene of An Englishman Abroad *[1983], when you see Guy Burgess marching across the bridge in Moscow in his Savile Row suit.*

It's not exactly the same.

No, but it's still a man marching off in a world of his own imagination.

Yes. Absolutely. That's what I loved about *Billy Liar*, though I think now we could have gone much further with the Walter Mitty–ish style of the film.

Done more with the fantasy scenes?

Probably. Handled them more wittily. I mean, it's quite funny to see him mow down his whole family in frustration, like a Che Guevara character.

It's a portrait of an artist, really.

Yes. Very much so. It's the portrait of somebody with imagination, which cannot express itself easily in the conventional suburbia that he comes from. But at the time when I made it, and after the success of *A Kind of Loving*, *Billy Liar* didn't really stand a chance by comparison. I always regarded my first film as a bigger success—I'm not so sure now.

Not necessarily the better film?

No. It's very difficult to not be affected by something that's successful as compared to something that's less commercial and doesn't find a vast amount of favor with the public. There's great pleasure in having something that works with an audience—I love it. It doesn't mean to say that it's necessarily a better film, but success is enjoyable.

How did Julie Christie come into the picture? Hers is a fairly small part but memorable. Did the part grow as you went along?

No, Julie was not cast originally. I was aware of her since I made *The Class*—the last documentary I made for

Monitor—because she was in another class and was very striking. I certainly remember seeing her wandering around the school. But to me, Liz in *Billy Liar* needed physically to be a big-breasted earth figure, and we cast somebody who was physically right, and I thought could bring it off. Her name was Topsy Jane. But she couldn't hack it. I realized that quite early on. I looked at Julie's test again and thought we were mad not to use her. So we changed and had to go back to Bradford and reshoot a month's work. That was the first time I ever had to make a casting change. The second was far more serious. We had considered Peter Finch for the role of the doctor in *Sunday Bloody Sunday*, but he wasn't free and turned us down without having read the script, so we cast Ian Bannen, which was, I'm afraid, in the circumstances, quite a mistake.

Billy Liar *made Julie Christie into a star.*

Yes, although she'd done leading roles, it certainly launched Julie.

Have you always been in control of your casting?

I have a casting director who makes suggestions. But I've been in control of the casting, because I go to all the sessions. I don't think I've always been accurate in summoning up the best person. There have been times when I've realized that probably a mistake was made—but not as devastating as if we'd gone on with Ian Bannen in *Sunday Bloody Sunday*.

You never felt that somebody was being foisted on you for commercial reasons?

Not in a disadvantageous way. I've had to cast a role because we had to find somebody who meant something at the box office and "opened the picture"—which is what they always say now: he or she could "open a picture." So there is a commercial element that I take seriously when casting. But I don't think the fact that you've got someone who's well-known and right for the part is going necessarily to turn a film into a great success. And sometimes you can get away with someone who's not right for the part but well-known because there's audience identification.

Julie Christie has a small part, and yet it leaves much more of an impact than the space it occupies in the film. What gives some actors such screen presence?

I think there is a mysterious process that goes on between a person and that piece of glass which is the lens. And I understand why a camera is considered an evil eye by orthodox Jews. I think it does take something from the person. Quite often after six takes or so, when you've said, "Right, let's move on," an actor will say, "Well, that was the one, wasn't it?" and I'd say, "Well, I don't know until I see the dailies. Until I see it up on the screen, I don't know." And that's true. There is something mysterious about the whole process and how a personality is seen on film. There are actors who work because of their personality and who aren't that versatile as performers. The reason they're popular and famous is that there is something about them as people that makes them stars. And they aren't that different in different parts. Alec Guinness was a prime example of the opposite, of somebody who didn't exploit his own personality, whatever that was, and gave some wonderful screen performances.

Where would you put Julie Christie in that respect?

I think Julie became a very much better actress with experience. I don't think she ever particularly wanted to become a star.

She's uncomfortable with it?

I adore her, and she's wonderful and original, and there are many kindnesses that I remember her doing. But I think Julie was uncomfortable having to live up to being a star. She got better at it the more big films she did, but I don't know that she really was ever very comfortable being a star.

Darling *[1965]*. *Some of that had to be redone, too, did it not?*

Darling started originally at a cricket match at Lords Cricket Ground, which was an awful sequence of untold stupidity, which we scrapped totally. We did come up with another idea long after the movie was done—we had some reshooting to do.

Frederic Raphael wrote the script?

Yes, Freddie Raphael and I worked together very happily to begin with. Then he went off and disappeared on holiday trips abroad, and we were in trouble. We got other writers involved. Freddie heard about this and took terrible umbrage. I was—and so was Joe Janni—very disappointed with the first script. It didn't seem to have much reality about it, and Joe insisted that we spend time with somebody he knew who was, in his mind, the sort of template for the Diana character, played by Julie Christie. So very reluctantly on Freddie's part, we spent time with this girl and talked to her a great deal about her life, her marriage—or several marriages, maybe—and out of that came several good ideas.

Why was he reluctant?

I think Freddie felt that we were all intent on destroying the writer's contribution, and he was rather grand about that. He was banging on about not needing to have experienced something to be able to put it down on paper. He said: "It should come from the imagination." Well, to a certain extent he's right, but at the same time I've always found— but that's part of my documentary background—that some amazing things can come from being with somebody, following their lives quite closely.

Indeed, we got into a lot of trouble because when we met this friend of Joe's, she told us an awful lot about her life and her husband, who was a bit of a stick-in-the-mud. At one time she wanted a divorce from him, and he knew she'd given a lot of detail about their lives to us, so she issued an injunction to stop us from putting it into the script.

She was a society lady?

Oh, yes, very much so.

Which the character in the film isn't really?

No—well, she aspires to it. In the end, I think we came up with a happy medium. But by that time Freddie had found out that other people had been brought in to rewrite certain things, and he wouldn't play ball. He was on a holiday in Greece, and the problem is that film doesn't stop for anybody. You know, if you're ill when something happens then you can postpone as much as you can and shoot round it, but inevitably a film production is like a runaway train.

Darling *is probably the most moralistic film that you've made. Diana is not an admirable or even especially sympathetic character. It's a kind of rake's-progress story, a morality tale.*

I remember when we were trying to get the money to make it, I was given a kind of interview by this group of people who were deciding whether they were going to put money into it or not. They said: "But why should we find her sympathetic?" So I said: "Well, one of the things she does is to make terrible mistakes, and that's entirely human, and I think that you can understand that." "Well, how are you going to show that?" "Well," I said, "have you ever heard of a close-up?"

Clearly, she makes some very mistaken choices. She ends up in a marriage that may be comfortable physically but doesn't leave her any more secure. In fact, it leaves her less secure than she was earlier in her adventures. But I have to admit that *Darling* is not my favorite film. Now why is that? I think perhaps because it's got a construction that can be seen as finger wagging, which is not really me at all.

You were quite tough on Julie Christie in Darling.

Was I?

There is the story that she didn't want to do the nude scene near the end and felt rather bullied into doing it.

She didn't want to do it, you are quite right. I mean, she was scared shitless of doing it because the camera was following her down a series of corridors and she was doing a sort of striptease until she ended up naked in front of the mirror in her bedroom. Julie also kept saying in the initial days of making *Darling:* "I wouldn't do that, that's not like me." And I said: "It's not you that you're playing. You are playing this character."

But I charmed her into it. Told her how important it was, which, looking back, I don't think was true. Thereby hangs a tale of censorship. The husband was played by José Luis de Villalonga, who was a Spanish poet and not really an actor at all, but I was intrigued by him, and I thought he would hit the right note.

What was the censorship tale?

Well, she ends up naked. But you didn't see anything. It was all implied, but when we printed what we got in the rushes, there was a tiny glimpse of one nipple. And the Americans were nothing if not prudish and ridiculous about sex. Somebody with Joe Levine's company, who was distributing the film, said we had to look very carefully at this sequence. He knew there was something there. I said you could only see it if you stopped the frame, and he said he couldn't allow it to go through. So I had to come out to America with the negative of the scene in my pocket, so they could blow it up and avoid the careless nipple that was popping into view. This is just one example of censorship.

What others are there?

There were scenes that they wanted out or changed, which upset me terribly because in the end I think it damaged the film. There was a scene, for example, where Julie Christie was taken by Laurence Harvey to a kind of brothel in Paris to watch a sex demonstration, and there is a girl in a mac waiting for her male partner to arrive. While they are drinking and having cigarettes, they offer her a Gauloise, and she says in French: "I'm sorry but I don't smoke." It was all built up to the entrance in a flustered manner of the male partner in this sex act, and as he starts to undress he apologizes for being late because he couldn't find a parking spot. Now I thought that was very funny, but the censor couldn't see it at all, and it was cut out.

Why did that have to be cut?

Because they thought it was, you know—in the end it was worse. Because there was no evidence of a male partner in the way it was cut, it looked as if they were waiting for her to masturbate. Even my mother, when she saw the original print, when we hadn't cut it out, said what a brilliant idea it was—not shocked at all. But I was told: "No, you can't have it."

Was there much of this kind of thing?

I'll always remember our brushes with the censor in the old days, when Joe Janni would submit the script to the censor's office, and they would tell you in advance what was not going to be allowed or would cause difficulty. There were something like thirty-three cuts in the script for *A Kind of Loving.*

To do with sex?

Yes. Buying condoms, for instance, was a no-no. John Trevelyan, the censor then, liked to be flattered and to be asked down to the studio for his advice. So we'd ask him for lunch at Shepperton, so he could watch the shooting of the scene where they look at nude girls in a book, when Alan Bates is trying to seduce June Ritchie. And he'd appear, kind of like a good voyeur, sitting near the camera, peering through his glasses and nodding sagely.

You use humor in violence, but a lot of the sex in your films is made to look funny, too.

Because I think sex *is* sort of funny. I think it's better to deal with it humorously. I love the buildup to Alan Bates's entrance, when he's going to seduce—or try and seduce—Ingrid in *A Kind of Loving*, and he's testing his breath and everything else in the mirror in the bathroom upstairs. I think that's funny.

Of course it's funny. But I think of some of the scenes in The Day of the Locust *[1975], which are truly very sexy and not meant to be funny. So you are good at it, but in most of your films you haven't really emphasized eroticism.*

Yes, I think that's true. I'm trying to think, What is erotic? I must have done something with Julie Christie that was erotic rather than funny? Perhaps I haven't.

Do you think it would have been different had you been, let's say, twenty years younger, and there would have been more freedom to explore homosexual eroticism, or do you think that doesn't really make a difference?

Well, there are homosexual scenes in *Sunday Bloody Sunday* that are not funny.

No, they're tender.

They're tender.

More than erotic.

Yes, I think they are that. Perhaps eroticism isn't something that I'm terribly interested in.

Maybe because you've been relatively content in real life?

Yes, but I've had quite an erotic real life.

You have been a pioneer in the history of cinema in that you are one of the first directors who has taken male love seriously. The first overtly gay character comes into Darling.

Yes, a rather camp photographer.

Did you want him to be a camp character?

I wanted him to be very relaxed in the part, so that he and she were great friends, and there were no secrets. They both went off in the film with the same pretty Italian waiter, which I thought was fun and all right.

Was this considered to be bold at the time?

I don't think so particularly. I got to that a bit later on when I felt that I should or could use a personal experience in my own life, which was the origin of *Sunday Bloody Sunday*. In fact, *Darling* got extremely well reviewed, by and large, in America particularly, for its honesty in dealing with all kinds of relationships. And I am very pleased with that side of the film.

We haven't really talked about the other two stars in Darling, *Dirk Bogarde and Laurence Harvey. How did you come to cast them?*

Originally the part that Dirk Bogarde played was written for an American, and I pursued Paul Newman like mad to do it. He was acting in a play on Broadway at the time, with his wife. I went to see him several times, and he proceeded to do a sort of striptease in the dressing room, which felt to me like a bit of a come-on, but in the end he turned me down. He said: "No, it's a supporting role, and good though I think it is, I don't want to do it." So that was that.

Could you say something about Dirk Bogarde as an actor?

The actors that I have loved working with, or wanted to work with, have all been people with a good deal of depth. You don't see everything they have got to give at one time. You know that there is a resonance about what they want. Peter Finch is a very good example of that and Alan Bates and Montgomery Clift. They have that wonderful quality of never showing you everything, and you knew that there was a reservoir of emotion and feeling that they had in reserve, and I have always thought that was a wonderful quality in film. Dirk Bogarde was not only wonderful in the role, but he was extremely nice to work with, particularly from Julie's point of view. He knew she was nervous and that she needed all the support she could get. He was absolutely sweet and generous with her. Which I can't really say about Laurence Harvey, who was perfectly happy to frighten her and keep her on a tight lead.

How did Laurence Harvey enter the picture?

We cast him long before we got to shoot him and work with him. He was in *Camelot* at the time in the Drury Lane theater, and when we were getting close to needing him, we got a message that he was not going to do it.

Larry was quite a theatrical character. You know: "Darling heart, what are you doing up at this time? You should be in bed." "Well," I said, "you know, I want you in the film." "Oh, darling, feel the weight of this costume, just feel the weight of it. I have to get in and out of this thing, I can't do it, I really can't." And besides, he said, "I have a lousy exit in the movie." So I said I happened to have another scene with me which I wanted him to read and see if that got him out of the picture in a better way. So he took it.

Did Raphael have to write this?

Yes, he did. In the end our relationship became really quite competitive. As a director, I don't find the writer's attitude that "all you're doing is wrecking my beautiful script" is terribly fair.

Yet he got the Oscar?

Julie was the only one who went out for the Oscar ceremony. Joe Levine, who was presenting the film and had taken over the final financing of it, gave a party in London for us. I went back to bed feeling a bit queasy and woke up in the morning with a terrible migraine, which I used to get in those days, with vomiting and everything else. I rang Joe Janni's wife, Stella, to find out if she'd heard any news about the Oscars. And she said that Julie Christie had won, and Freddie Raphael had won, and the costume designer had won, but I hadn't. And I said that I wasn't surprised, but how terrific, I must ring Freddie. I dialed his number. It was early in the morning and I felt I was about to vomit. I got him on the line and said: "Congratulations! It is terrific, and I'm so pleased for you, and I'd better go . . . arrrrgh."

———————

Far from the Madding Crowd. *What made you decide to make a film about a very English literary classic?*

This dates back to the time we were doing the final mix of *Darling,* and Julie Christie was under contract to Joe Janni for more films. And while we were waiting for the reels to be changed and all the sound tracks to be put up, we were discussing what next to do with Julie. The editor, Jim Clark, suggested that she would be very good in a Thomas Hardy subject.

Why **Far from the Madding Crowd?**

Tess of the D'Urbervilles, which Roman Polanski did again later, had been done by MGM some years before. So when I was sailing back from New York by sea after the whole business of opening *Darling,* I decided to read *Far from the Madding Crowd*—which I didn't know. By the time we got to Southampton, I'd made up my mind that this would be a good movie. And totally different in feeling. I didn't want to come out of the same bolt-hole again. I just recognized that the theme was very strong and the writing very, very good. So we plunged in.

I wonder why Jim Clark suggested Hardy in particular.

I think that if Thomas Hardy had been writing today, he would have written some very good film scripts, because he was such a visual writer, with a sense of drama and dramatic irony. There is a particular sequence in *Far from the Madding Crowd* that I loved doing. Bathsheba spends all night out in the wood, because she had made such a mess of things, she felt she didn't want to go home. And in the morning she wakes up, in a bit of a state. She hears and sees—this is in the book and the film—a boy walking across the fields with his satchel, trying to remember his lesson for school. She realizes he is in a state, and that makes her own problems seem less . . . it evens them out. It's so beautifully observed by Hardy; we filmed it more or less as written.

You were criticized at the time, I believe, for the casting in Far from the Madding Crowd. *Terence Stamp was perhaps not good enough, although he looked marvelous, and Julie Christie wasn't really right because she was too much of a 1960s figure.*

But she's playing a modern girl—I mean that was the whole point of casting her.

So you don't really regret that?

No, I don't regret that. I think that was something the critics reached for, saying, "She's too modern," but I disagree with them. I thought that she was a modern woman to the extent that she was left the farm and decided that she would go through with it, and run it, which was unheard of then.

I didn't think Stamp was very good. We had a bad experience with each other—he didn't like working with me, either. Some of it worked. But I remember we had to dub a lot of his performance because he just didn't have enough balls. When he turns up unexpected at Boldwood's party and dance, he had the line: "Bathsheba, I've come to take you home," and if anything needed power behind it, it was that, and I never thought that Terry got it. And because I didn't think he had it, I suppose I must have given myself away. To be a director, you have to be a very good actor, because you've got to leave actors with a shred of pleasure at doing what they're doing, and if they think you admire them and like them in the role, that's all for the good.

But Julie Christie worked?

She did worry about her performance. I remember once we were doing the pay scene, where they all gather, and she summons them up. It's quite a funny scene—rather charming—and Julie was stumbling, I don't know why. And I said: "Are you all right, dear, you seem very thrown by something." I asked if it was that time of the month or whatever, because I seriously thought that something was wrong, and she said: "Oh, but they're all so good, they're so good." So I said: "Well, forget that—you're good, too, so forget it. You cannot think in those negative terms." So she tried to forget it, but I don't think she did really. And they *were* all good; it was a wonderful cast, all those people whom we cast as workers on the farm.

Peter Finch was wonderful, too.

One of the reasons why I think Dirk Bogarde soured on me—this is possible—is that Joe Janni opened his big mouth and said to Dirk: "The next film we're doing, there's a marvelous part for you," which was Boldwood. But I disagreed with him. I said there was an actor that would be even better—Peter Finch.

Dirk Bogarde wanted to do it?

Since he had been told that he was going to do it, and I made no move, he assumed that I didn't rate him. In fact, he used to say that.

You never worked with him again, did you? But remained friends?

Well, up to a point, until he came years later for dinner. He'd left France and was a bitter man. And we all—his old friends—said we've got to have Dirk round for dinner and see that he's all right and not lonely. So I don't think he wanted for invitations. My situation had changed with the great commercial success of *Midnight Cowboy*, so I was able to indulge in my passion for collecting and that kind of thing, and I lived in a very beautiful house. And he arrived, looked around, and said: "This is the house of a rich man—and you've had nothing but flops!" I was never very well disposed toward him since.

The film had a mixed reception.

I'm critical of the film—I think it's terribly slow. I think I was in the habit of liking the leisurely pace and starting on a detail of a building or something and then panning down and opening the whole thing up to a street, or whatever it was, and this made it frightfully slow. Freddie Raphael, who wrote the script, pointed this out afterward. We were too much in awe of Thomas Hardy, and we should have taken more liberties in the screenplay, as we did later with *The Day of the Locust*. We took quite a lot of liberties with that story—made a story out of it. But the experience of living in Dorset and making the film there was a pleasurable one. I lived in half a farmhouse near the coast outside Weymouth. And I decided I wanted to have a place in the country. I still enjoy it and appreciate the isolation of being in the country more than an urban existence.

Even though you're not very often on your own? You're not very good at being on your own.

No, not terribly good at being on my own. I mean, I can do it, but I don't want to do it for a prolonged time. I don't like being on my own.

You went to America for the opening of Far from the Madding Crowd. *I don't believe it was a happy introduction to Hollywood, was it?*

Not at all. We sensed how it was going down before we ever arrived there. We had one of those big charity premieres in New York, which was awful to get through, particularly as the audience really weren't liking the movie. And in the interval my agent and everybody else had obviously read the *New York Times* notice, which beat us into the tarmac of Broadway. My parents, who are civilians in this business, were wise enough to say, Darling, I don't think we'll come to the premiere party, which was just as well, because there was an enormous amount of empty tables in the Plaza Hotel. I think there were three tables that had people at them when we walked in, and everybody tried to look sporting and applaud, but it was an absolute disaster.

This is the dark side of America?

Well, it's the dark side of showbiz. It's an awful business. I was going on to L.A. the next day, and I didn't sleep very much. It was my first visit to the West Coast, and there was a rather well-known actor across the aisle reading the notice in *The New York Times,* and I thought how awful, I am branded. The man sitting next to me on the plane was head of publicity at MGM and he said: "What is this *Midnight Cowboy*? Be very careful what you do next—you can't afford to make something which is really not right for you."

LIBERATION

Most people, including John Schlesinger himself, consider *Midnight Cowboy* (1969) and *Sunday Bloody Sunday* (1971) to be his best films. John was also very fond of *The Day of the Locust* (1975), which has a cult following today but had a mixed reception when it was first released.

Midnight Cowboy was adapted for the screen from James Leo Herlihy's novel by Waldo Salt. The stars were Dustin Hoffman and Jon Voight. It won Academy Awards for best director, best picture, and best adapted screenplay.

Sunday Bloody Sunday was written by Penelope Gilliatt in close but not always happy cooperation with John. The three protagonists of the love story were played by Peter Finch, Glenda Jackson, and Murray Head. It won the David di Donatello Award in Italy and the British Academy Awards for best director, best film, best actor, and best actress.

Nathanael West's story about the seamy side of Hollywood, *The Day of the Locust,* was adapted for the screen by Waldo Salt and featured Donald Sutherland, Karen Black, and William Atherton. Perhaps John's darkest picture— made at the happiest time of his life—it failed to win a major award.

In 1972, John directed his only musical, *I and Albert,* at the Piccadilly Theatre in London. He also directed three plays for the National Theatre: *Heartbreak House* (1975), *Julius Caesar* (1977), and *True West* (1981).

In 1972, John contributed a segment to *Visions of Eight,* a documentary by eight directors on the Munich Olympic Games.

In 1970, John received a CBE (Commander of the British Empire) from the Queen.

What happened on your first visit to Hollywood?

We arrived in Hollywood to be met by some faceless publicity executives from MGM, who said: "You must be very tired. We've canceled the party for the opening tonight." It didn't take me long to realize that they had dumped us because the film clearly wasn't going to be successful. I was miserable and wanted every weekend to escape from Los Angeles and go to San Francisco.

Why?

Because San Francisco felt much more European.

Were you working on the script of Midnight Cowboy?

Not yet. MGM didn't want any part of it. They were advising me to run. I couldn't face working on anything. I was very upset by the failure and continued to leave town and go up to San Francisco. But mostly I had to stick around in L.A.

Why?

Because MGM got a famous editor to take as much stuff out of the film [*Far from the Madding Crowd*] as she could. And when I saw it, I was horrified because they had taken out all the texture, so I went to the head of MGM and said, "Look, we can do a much better job. We know what you are trying to do, but the wrong things have been selected to go." So Jim Clark and I hacked away and needed to remix and everything else. We altered some of the music, but it didn't make any difference.

How drastically did they alter the film?

We had to take out about twenty minutes. Or that's what they were aiming at. I can't remember the details because I was so angry and so upset to find that people had been tampering, and lies were being told. But gradually I got back into working again and got over my disappointment, as you have to. You can't allow one failure to really undo you.

You met Michael Childers, your partner, round about then?

Yes, we were introduced by a wonderful comedienne, who did several musicals, called Kaye Ballard. I never thought then that our relationship was going to continue for thirty-four years, minimally, because I had never had a relationship of any kind of length, duration, or intensity, and it started very gently. But it's gone on.

While working on the script of *Cowboy,* we rented a house at Malibu on the beach, which was gorgeous—to be there in November, hearing how damp it was over in England, and we were having beautiful sunny days on the beach.

How did Midnight Cowboy *first come to you?*

A great friend of mine, a painter, had read the book and told me to read it with a view of perhaps making a film. So I did and indeed felt that if I was going to come to America to make a film, this would be the ideal subject for me. It was fairly candid. I thought the characters were fascinating, very alien to anything I had experienced. So we commissioned a screenplay.

From Waldo Salt?

Yes. Waldo, who'd suffered a great deal during the blacklist period of McCarthy, was a highly intelligent, resourceful writer and had some wonderful ideas. But he was a very strange man to work with because he'd make a date to meet up, and we expected him to have done a certain number of pages, and he'd say: "It's all in my head but I haven't actually got it on paper yet." We'd either cancel the meeting or see where we'd got theoretically, and gradually the script evolved.

You say this was a very alien world. But how much of a stranger to this world were you? You must have seen at least a bit of this life in L.A. or New York.

The New York streets and Forty-second Street and people high on drugs of one sort or another, all this was a reasonably new experience for me. But, yes, a lot of what's in the film we'd observed or I'd observed not only in New York but also Los Angeles. I don't think I would have dreamed them up, because I wouldn't have known how to do that.

You talked about meeting a woman who was not unlike Diana in Darling. *Had you actually talked to hustlers about their lives?*

I met a hustler at a dinner party. He had been invited because I was looking for an adviser to help me with the street scenes. So we put him on the film. Still, the film nearly didn't happen a number of times. There were great arguments with United Artists about how to reduce the cost because they were nothing if not conscious of the price of film.

Were there moral objections from the studio?

No, United Artists was a very extraordinary organization, because once they had agreed on the director, they believed in letting him have his way. They trusted me, and that doesn't often happen.

How did you find Dustin Hoffman? Wasn't it right after he did The Graduate?

Yes, but when we were discussing casting, Jerry Hellman, the producer, said: "I wish you'd seen Hoffman off Broadway giving the performance in Henry Living's play *Eh?*, which is remarkable, because he's totally different. You've got to meet him, since your only knowledge of him is *The Graduate*." He was right, and I went to New York, and Hoffman very sensibly had dressed in the sort of clothes that he imagined Ratso might have to hang around Forty-second Street—dirty raincoat and stuff like that. And to Forty-second Street we went, and there he was kind of auditioning—not really, but yes, *really*—because he wanted to play the part and knew I didn't know him as a character actor. We spent much of the night wandering around Forty-second Street and the pool halls and restaurants in Hell's Kitchen. And then Hoffman starting to limp along Forty-second Street, and he seemed to sort of vanish into the background, which was exactly what I wanted to see—well, that's what he made me see.

So he was convincing?

Absolutely.

Didn't he rather regret it when the film came out? I seem to recall that he felt it wasn't good for his image to play this scummy character.

We had a screening for the cast and crew when it was almost done. It was a Sunday, and I remember this very well—
it was my birthday, and I was having a party in the
evening—and Hoffman came, said very little at the end, and
didn't come to the party afterward. He sent his manager with
a nice book and a message. And I asked what he thought of
the film, and the manager said: "Well, I think you'd better
talk to him personally about that." So Jon Voight and I went
to his Third Avenue apartment and although he said, "No,
it's all right, it's fine, it's good," he clearly was upset by something, and I've never really to this day been able to put my
finger on it. I thought his performance was absolutely wonderful and had said so, but he seemed, as actors quite often
are when they first see something, to be disappointed. I think
he expected more from the film and himself.

*He never acknowledged that perhaps it was one of his finest
performances?*

No, he did, he did later. I don't know what it was. I have
a feeling that he felt Jon Voight had run away with the film,
which he didn't, though he was brilliant in it, in a much less
easy part. I just don't know what had got into him, but something had. One day, when we were recording, doing the post
sync, I called him. He was very excited, and he said: "Show
me some more, show me some more." So I ran him a reel or
two, and he got straight on the phone to his manager and
said: "Come over quickly. You must see a little bit of this
film, it's so good." And the manager came over, and the only

question he asked was: "When in the film does this appear?"
He was obviously calculating what sort of length the part
was and how much impression Hoffman would make. Oh,
the relationship with actors and managers and agents and
things is a terrible problem sometimes.

*The dialogues in the film look so natural. How much of this
came out of improvisation?*

There are certain actors who are very good at improvis-
ing, like Dustin Hoffman and Glenda Jackson. There is a sequence in *Midnight Cowboy* where they're cooking and
eating in their cold-water flat, and Hoffman's character is
provoking the cowboy and says: "You're beginning to smell"
and that kind of thing. We had to investigate the nature of
two people living together, starting off in a rather hostile
fashion—not trusting each other, eventually beginning to
break that reserve down, and knowing each other much better, and starting to overtly criticize each other as part of the
living-together process. And there was quite a lot of improvisation. We taped all this and then got it transcribed and
picked the best lines or ideas or ways to take a scene. I've
done that many times, and it can improve the script but also
wreck a perfectly good scene.

*The opening sequence of the film. Is that when you see the
cowboy boots walking along the street . . . ?*

No, that isn't the opening shot. The opening shot is a
white screen and the drive-in cinema and the little kid play-

ing. That was a synthesis of ideas, which didn't come until we had shot the New York end of the film—which was a lot—and then got to Texas. We were going round possible locations, and the idea of a sequence in a drive-in cinema occurred to Michael Childers, who was my assistant on this film. But it was rather an involved light sequence, with lots of cars and film scenes from windscreens and things, and we decided it was too costly and a too lumbering, rather literal way of doing things. So we decided to do it with sound and just the image of this boy on a rocking horse under the screen by day, with nobody else around.

As a fake cowboy?

A fantasy. And to convey the idea of cowboys and Indians—although the nature of his cowboying is very, very different.

A lot is compressed in the opening scenes of the film.

I think that the condensing of time to tell the story is quite an important thing to start learning early, and I've used time lapses in that way quite often. The construction at the beginning of the film starts with Joe Buck as a little kid and his fascination with the cinema. Then it jumps to him leaving his home. An enormous amount of time is used in a kind of flashback, which I think was effective. [The song performed by Harry Nilsson] was tremendously useful in conveying both the rhythm and the attitude. The lyrics were very, very hard to beat. It added a very great deal—"Everybody's talking at me, I don't hear a word they're saying, Only the echoes of my mind." The lyrics have everything to do with the success of the use of that song, as does the rhythm.

It wasn't composed for the film?

No, it wasn't. And that was a problem, because United Artists wanted to own the copyright of the song, which of course they wouldn't have done. So they sent someone else to do a song, who was hopeless. Then John Barry, the composer, came aboard to work not only on the score and the choice of music that we wanted for the album but to write a song with Harry Nilsson, which became something of a hit. It's called "I Guess the Lord Must Be in New York City," which had a similar rhythm, lyrically wasn't bad, but didn't have the sort of poetic quality of "Everybody's Talkin'." So we turned it down.

Didn't Bob Dylan write something as well?

"Lay Lady Lay." It was something we considered. Joni Mitchell was another, who wrote far too many words describing the situation, when really what one wanted was attitude.

You have an extraordinary eye for the American landscape. I'm thinking of the way you see the bus going through this cluttered countryside. There are a lot of little satirical points, which remind me of your documentary style, like seeing the billboard that says: "If you don't have an oil well . . . , get one!" Or in New York City, where you show somebody lying on the street in front of Tiffany's, with everybody stepping over him. Are there times when you feel, looking back, that you tarted up reality a bit too much?

I've never felt that using something with tongue in cheek has been a bad thing. Humor of a sort is never very far away, I hope, because I like to look at things with an amused eye, because that is what I am. There are lots of things that make me smile, not necessarily laugh out loud. But no, I don't think that I've overdone it. Why choose Tiffany's? I suppose for that very reason. It's on the corner of two very prominent New York streets, and it's the kind of thing that one would see. I'd certainly seen incidents in major streets in New York, and that's one of the reasons why I enjoy America, because in Britain we live a somewhat secluded life. We don't let everything hang out like the Americans do. But I rather like that; it's all grist to the mill, it's all stuff that you can use. I think that perhaps one has dotted "i"s and crossed "t"s too obviously sometimes. Symbolism perhaps is a bit in your face, and I've tried my best to control that as best I can, as I've grown older, and thought that one could approach something with a little more subtlety.

I remember you once telling me that the very last shot of the film, when you see Joe Buck with the dead Ratso in his arms, was cut just as rain started splashing the window.

The cameraman had stopped shooting.

But that might have been a good thing.

Well, it might. But I was upset that he didn't continue.

You don't think that would have been laying it on a bit thick?

It might have been if it had suddenly rained at that moment. But yes, I would have certainly shot it, but it wasn't worth re-creating by technical means. It certainly would have made a very strong end to the film.

If I have a criticism of *Cowboy,* it's that I think it's terribly snazzy in the way it's cut. I wonder if I were approaching it now whether I wouldn't do it in a simpler fashion. Maybe not, but I felt terribly confident in those days—jump cuts and all sorts of things. I think I've calmed down a bit since then. I don't know whether that's necessarily a good thing.

It's a sign both of the time it was made and your own age when you made it.

Yes. But I wasn't that young—I was in my forties.

Yes, you were in your forties, but it was a snazzy age.

I suppose so, and it seemed to work. People were taken by surprise. I remember the British critics. "Schlesinger Released" was one of the things that I read.

I think *Cowboy* needed an energetic approach. *Sunday Bloody Sunday,* which came afterward, had a much more classical style to it.

**Midnight Cowboy *doesn't have that rake's-progress element
of showing somebody getting his comeuppance as Diana
does in* Darling. *Joe Buck ends up, I think, being redeemed.***

Yes, which we also got quite a lot of flak for. I'll never forget the first screening at the Berlin Film Festival. As soon as
the film ended there was an outbreak of booing, which made
us look at each other with some surprise. When my name was
mentioned and I came onstage, they went, "Boo, Boo!" The
screening was followed by a question-and-answer session for
the press, and they were very rude about us: "How can you
make a film about a hustler, when there's the whole of Viet-
nam going on? How can you even think of doing a movie of
this sort?" And so on and so forth. It was heavily political.

A rather stupid attitude.

Oh, absolutely stupid. I think the reason why *Midnight
Cowboy* has lasted is not only because it's a good story but
because it does have a deep human quality which people
have gathered from the film and admired in it and has given
the film this extraordinary long life. That is also why it
doesn't seem to have dated terribly. There are dated sequences in it, but I'm not sure that *Darling* hasn't dated a
great deal more.

Women are not viewed with great sympathy.

I don't know really. I never thought of it like that. I never
thought of it as misogynistic. The cowboy has this fantasy,

which is pretty politically incorrect, that he can go to New York and become a hustler for rich women and is God's gift to them because his sexual prowess is the one thing that he's got in his favor, if favor it is. That attitude toward women as objects may have worked for the late sixties, but it doesn't do so now.

No, but the only tenderness you see in the film is between the men. The women are all ball breakers or whores of one kind or another.

Well, I was thinking of his grandmother, the little flashes we see.

Well, she's not an advertisement for womankind either!

I'd never thought of it as misogynistic, but perhaps it is, because the story is of this relationship between the two men. It was not viewed kindly in, as it were, gay society. It was viewed as somewhat antigay, which I'd never intended.

Whereas in fact it's a celebration of male love.

Yes, but I think if you look at it with a sort of gay sensibility and want everything to be positive about gay life, it could be interpreted as antigay.

Was this one of the reasons you were attracted to the subject—that it's a celebration of love between two men?

Yes, it probably was. It was a theme that had never been really tackled before.

It's odd in fact that from the gay point of view people wouldn't have understood the power of Midnight Cowboy. The reception of Sunday Bloody Sunday [1971], which revolves around an explicitly gay relationship, seems to have done much better in this regard.

Sunday Bloody Sunday was very well received, as far as I was concerned. *Midnight Cowboy, Sunday Bloody Sunday,* and *The Day of the Locust* were all made cheek by jowl. This was probably the moment I felt most liberated, when I felt I could make films on these sorts of subjects. Perhaps I've never reached that point since, though I'm very happy with my two Alan Bennett pieces, *An Englishman Abroad* and *A Question of Attribution,* which I really enjoyed making for the BBC.

Could a film like Midnight Cowboy be made again?

I don't think it could.

Why?

Because I think film has become so expensive to make and sell. I don't think they'd be prepared to take the sort of risks that they did then.

With the subject?

I think it would be very difficult. That doesn't mean to say there aren't some outrageous films these days that are very funny and very candid. The extraordinary thing is that America is such a self-righteous country. Sex—what you can show of it, compared with violence, which I think is much more dangerous—is something people here are very scared of.

Is America more puritanical about sex than England?

Oh, very much so, no question, yes, don't you think?

It seems like a strangely mixed picture to me, because there is that deep reservoir of puritanism, while on the other hand America can be very wild and pushes things further, in certain circles anyway, than other countries. After all, the kind of things you saw on Hollywood Boulevard or Forty-second Street you wouldn't have seen in most European cities, at least not on that scale. It was the beginning of an explosion of gay life, which didn't take place in quite the same way or so soon in other countries. Perhaps the wildness and the puritanism are two sides of the same coin?

Well, I do know that there's a marked difference in what you deal with in sex compared to violence. They are poles apart in America, and this has always worried me. Because it seems to me that when it comes to overt violence and overt sex, I know which one I think is more harmful or potentially more harmful.

Do you think that the famous kiss scene between the two male lovers in Sunday Bloody Sunday *would have been harder to shoot if it had been for an American studio?*

Yes, I do. My last film, starring Madonna and Rupert Everett, dealt with a gay man having a child with one woman, thinking that he'd had the child with another. The objections to what we showed in that film at the script stage were ridiculous, absolutely ridiculous. There was a sort of prurient censorship, which made mincemeat of the honesty of what we were trying to say in the film.

That was in 1999.

1999, yes.

⸻

You had not yet "come out" in 1970. How did you handle this when you made Sunday Bloody Sunday? *How aware were the people you worked with that this was an intensely personal project? Or was that never a problem?*

Well, I didn't let it be a problem. I'd become accustomed to the idea of including the subject in a movie. I had no problem with it. It didn't worry me when I came onto the set ready to do a scene.

It was the others who worried?

Oh, they were worried. And certainly I remember the first screening for United Artists, with all the high-ups there. We'd filled the little theater with secretaries and assistants and all that kind of thing, because I didn't want it just to be the suits who were watching the movie. And there was a lot of lighting up of cigarettes and wobbling of knee joints, and they were obviously embarrassed. At the end the reaction was not good. There was a very good reaction from some people, but the publicity department, which had seen us right through *Midnight Cowboy* with huge enthusiasm, met me after the screening and said, "Well, you've given us a hard one, John."

United Artists was a place in which everybody left their doors open, and you wandered around the passages, and if they were busy they'd wave you away, or if they weren't they'd say, "Come in." Well, on this occasion, after the screening, a lot of doors were closed. I suppose I should have expected it. They must have known, when they saw it, that they were in the presence of quite a bold film that dared to tread where nobody really had gone in such an overt fashion.

What was most shocking to people at the time?

There are several scenes with Peter Finch and Murray Head together naked, which people find shocking. And to this day the kiss between the two men causes a sort of gasp. I think that what caused people embarrassment is that we just let it happen. It was in the original script but written so that it tried to make light of it, tried to make it almost disappear, as if it wasn't happening. Penelope Gilliatt, who wrote the screenplay, and I basically disagreed about this. I didn't think that it should be portrayed with any kind of apology. She wanted it done in a long shot, with the two of them kissing in silhouette and all that kind of thing. I wanted the doctor to greet his lover, as if it were the normal thing to do. I said that if we started putting it in silhouette and long shot, it's special pleading and coy. I wanted them to be absolutely overt about it and unembarrassed. And they did, and they did it beautifully.

Neither of them was gay?

No. I first offered Paul Scofield the part that Peter Finch played, but he turned it down in a letter in which he said, "I don't suppose you want to know the reasons that I don't want to do this." I imagine it might have had something to do with the character's sexuality, but I could be wrong.

He never told you?

No. You know, you don't really want to know because it might put them in an embarrassing situation if they don't feel that they want to tell you.

And Ian Bannen, whom you cast first?

I don't think it was anything to do with the character being gay that really made Bannen nervous, but he didn't have that generous quality which we badly needed. Because the great thing about *Sunday Bloody Sunday* is that as a doctor one had to feel that his arms were outstretched, as though he were saying: "Trust me, come to me, and I will look after you." Then, when we put it right, and Peter Finch came over to do it, I was worried about the age difference between Peter Finch and Murray Head. So I tried to get someone to creep up behind and get a photograph of them together. When Peter saw this, he said: "No, no, no photographs—you either want me or you don't." And I said: "Well, there's just a discrepancy about the—" "I'm sorry—make up your mind." This kind of pushed us to the brink, but as soon as we started filming with him we realized we were on the right track, and everybody settled down and relaxed, and there was no more question.

How did the crew react to the love scenes?

The camera operator was horrified and went kind of "Yuck!" behind the camera and took his eye off the viewfinder. In fact, Billy Williams, the director of photography, came up to me before we'd even embarked on the film. He said: "I feel awkward taking this job." I asked him to be more explicit, and he said: "Well, it's the subject." I said: "Look, it's a question of how it's handled." So he stayed on board, and I will never forget the screening for the camera boys, when we finished the movie, and they brought their wives and they said: "Oh, it's a wonderful film, and I see what you were getting at, and it's not in the least offensive," and I was delighted.

Even the scene of the doctor picking up a rent boy on Piccadilly is shown in a very straightforward and rather natural way. You don't feel that you are seeing anything that's particularly outrageous. It's just another part of life.

That's quite deliberate.

Of course, but I think that's what makes this film so unusual.

Maybe for the time it was made. There's nothing I would change now in any of the films I've done that touch the subject, but some people in the gay community did say of *Sunday Bloody Sunday* that they wished I'd been a little more down and dirty with it, that I should have dealt with the pox, which people were still catching through unsafe sex. I saw what they meant. To them, it was all too much in good taste, perhaps, which is something I've been often accused of, because I have good taste, which perhaps is too—

Yes, except I'm not sure that I would agree with that comment. It is precisely because you presented these people's lives as utterly normal that it made such an impression. If it had been made more down and dirty or more camp, it would have lost that effect. Either people would have been prurient, or it would have been scandalous in the wrong way.

I think there's a question of degree. I don't mean that we should have really made it much more outrageous. I think we went far enough. We didn't have to see them actually indulging in whatever sexual practice they wanted to. But I would have liked more humor. I though that the Peter Finch character was a little bit of a saint. He wasn't, I know, in real life, because it was based on a relationship that I had had with an enchanting person. We laughed so much at the situation together. Then he'd go off the next weekend with his girlfriend.

And you're no saint.

I'm certainly no saint—didn't pretend to be.

There is quite a lot of humor in it, anyway. There are funny moments.

What I mean is that I wished we'd treated, or they as characters had treated, the situation they were in with more humor—perhaps more camp. I mean, there they were carrying on in this remarkable way. . . .

The Murray Head character is in a curious way a little bit like Karen Black, the starlet in The Day of the Locust, *in that people lust after him or want him, and in the end you feel he may not really be worth the candle, because he's a rather shallow figure.*

Which is why in the monologue, right at the end of the film, Finch turns to the camera and says, You know, you can criticize me, maybe he wasn't worth going through all this, but I thought he was—or words to that effect. It was that monologue—both the idea of it and the writing of it—that made me finally convinced that we could lick any other problems there were. When I read that in the script, on the plane going to New York, I thought that was a terrific scene. A very good way to end the film and original, and I thought I had to make this movie.

At what stage in the making of the film did you shoot that scene?

It was pretty near the end, because we had to destroy the set while the camera was making this continual move. I don't know how Finch played it with all the kerfuffle going on, bits of carpet being removed, furniture shifting, camera moving, and his concentration was extraordinary, because you were never made aware that it was a technically difficult scene to shoot, and it took all day. But it was very beautifully done. Somewhere someone has a record of it. I had the thought that it might be worth filming us filming it as an interesting document to have—and someone's run off with it.

One thing almost everybody who's seen the film remembers is the sound of Cosi Fan Tutti, *when the doctor is on his own in his house.*

Yes, the trio from the first act, which also lyrically has something—though you would never expect an audience to realize that.

No, but it's the mood of the music and watching him alone.

Yes. Yes, I like that. Anyway, I think *Sunday Bloody Sunday* was a film—perhaps because it's quite bourgeois, the people are all sort of very upper-middle—that was never really taken seriously in what's laughingly known as "queer cinema." I'm not sure that it's been taken as seriously as I hoped.

But that's because people are shortsighted and have no imagination. I think in the history of dealing with the sub-

*ject of homosexuality, it's a more important film than al-
most anything else.*

Well, I like to think so.

———

With **The Day of the Locust** *you still had carte blanche to do
what you liked?*

Yes, we sort of did. It was very difficult to get set up. The
book—the Nathanael West novella—was probably the best
piece of writing that I have ever read on the subject of Hollywood and the thirties, and I was very anxious to make the
film. But when the idea was first suggested to me, it was
long before I'd had a measure of success, and there was no
way that we were going to get it financed. So I had to bide
my time, really. And when I finally had a chance to make it,
Robert Evans—who ran Paramount—absolutely hated the
idea of *The Day of the Locust* and said so forcibly and did
anything that he could to prevent the film being made.

Why?

Essentially Bob Evans is a Hollywood man. He was head
of a studio, and he was about to produce his first film, *Chinatown*, with Roman Polanski directing. I think he just
didn't like what the film stood for. People in the industry
didn't like the story; they didn't like the rather downbeat,
critical attitude of West's novel. Evans also didn't think it
was commercial, which, of course, it wasn't. I still think it's

probably one of my better and consistent efforts, true to the spirit of the novel.

How much did you depart from the novel?

We changed quite a lot of it in detail. The passing of responsibility, which was an important sequence in the film, perhaps wasn't intended by West to be treated in the way that we did. One of my favorite bits of the film is the discussion after the set of the Battle of Waterloo collapses, because precautions had not been sufficiently taken. The discussion in the studio barbershop between the studio executives, which had no presence in the book, was a delicious extension that Waldo Salt and I had great pleasure in putting in. After all, Waldo had no happy memories of Hollywood, because he was blacklisted, so I suppose anything that came close to a kind of truth about passing the buck, which is typical of a studio system, was something we felt justified in including.

The Day of the Locust *must be the most lavish film you have made in terms of production values.*

Yes, it was. It was big, certainly. And it was made in America—in Hollywood. And it was marvelous working with a designer like Richard MacDonald, who's sort of dismissive of the studios, of the powers that be, because he is like a Captain Shotover: "What, what, don't need to bother about them." I adored working with him, because not only did he add a great deal to the production but he instinctively knew about film, although he originally began as a painter. He saw things in camera terms. I'd never worked with a designer who felt so at home with a camera—it was quite extraordinary.

When you conceived of the way The Day of the Locust *should look, did you ever think of the German expressionist movies that you saw as a child? I'm saying this because the film has a kind of grotesque quality that's not entirely dissimilar from prewar German films.*

Well, no, I'll tell you what we did. We were very concerned about the look of our film being good and catching with Conrad Hall, our brilliant cameraman, the look of Hollywood, which was glossy but at the same time dangerous. We wanted it to be alluring. I didn't want it to look too highly colored. Still now I cling to the impressionism of black and white and want the audience to provide something of their imagination when they're watching the movie. I don't like beautiful color, necessarily, but I do think it can be controlled. One of the films that I admired tremendously was Bertolucci's *The Conformist.*

The muted colors.

Yes, and also very controlled colors. I showed the entire crew, from designers to prop managers, *The Conformist* and said: "I want our film to take on this kind of look," and everybody understood that.

The other thing I've been fussy about—well, particular is a better word—is the casting of extras. There are some remarkable extras in *The Day of the Locust* with wonderful faces, and there you can use professional extras, which on the whole I hate, you know, because they look like extras.

Did Robert Evans come round to the project?

Even though he had been resolutely opposed to the making of *Locust*, he wanted *Chinatown* to look more like our film. And because of his position as head of Paramount he was entitled to look at our dailies. Both Jerry [Hellman] and I felt this was unforgivable, and as one producer to another Jerry insisted that there had to be a different set of boundaries, and we locked the cutting room and left the dailies in there, so they couldn't be screened for the studio, and it really became very, very unpleasant. The only person who wouldn't have any part of this was Polanski.

Anyway, we made the film, we cut it. And Bob, again as head of the studio, wanted to see the rough cut. Afterward, he invited me for lunch at his house and said that he never wanted this film to be made, that he still didn't like it, but that it was a very good achievement for what it was.

Then he remembered there were more characters in the screenplay. What had I cut? I was amazed that he was able to remember anything of the script. I told him that we'd cut quite a lot of the dwarf, the little person. And he said: "Sometimes you can make a film too short, and you're cutting out an important part of the fabric of the film, and that will harm it. I think you should put it back."

So we did, and it was much improved with this character intact in it.

And you worked with Evans again.

I was so amazed and impressed by Bob's executive attitude, which I wasn't in the habit of hearing, that when the book *Marathon Man* arrived through my letter box I took it very seriously. I thought, Well, I'd like to work with this man, although he was laughed at and mocked and imitated mercilessly—because he was a sort of flamboyant and amusing figure.

Did it take long to get the rhythm of the picture right?

Well, I'm not one for wanting to see the film put together very early on. I don't like seeing assembled footage when I'm shooting, on the whole. I'm terribly neurotic about it because it always seems to be terrible. When we were doing *The Day of the Locust,* I remember we all went off to Palm Springs for Christmas. And Jim Clark, the editor, said: "I want you to see the film," and I said, "Oh, God, no. Do I have to?" "Yes, I think you must." "Why?" "Well, I think there are things that you might learn from it."

So reluctantly I saw the film put together as far as they'd got, and I realized that it was terribly slow and that it needed a boot in the arse—badly. So I went back to shoot, and they found a different director! "Too slow, too slow!" and I was like a madman. Actors, you know, think and speak, whereas we speak as we think, it's all going on at once. And the way we speak and the pattern of speech has a sort of musical variation, and that's what's interesting. It's terribly boring if everything's done in the same way. So I came back like a dervish, saying, "Speak faster!" But I'm glad, because it rescued the film to a certain extent.

How did you choose the music in The Day of the Locust?

The choice of music is frightfully important, and I try things out with early cuts. I usually have some sort of music or sound track when I'm going into the cutting room or certainly very early on. I choose music that will reflect what I want as a pointer, if nothing else, to the composer.

In *The Day of the Locust* I needed some strangely atmospheric and tough, violent music for the last sequence, so we put on some Górecki. The feeling was right, and I said to John Barry, the composer: "Now make something like this." Then he rewrote, recomposed the section and rerecorded it and could hear what worked and what didn't work from an original piece of composed music. I love the moment when the film is seen through someone else's eyes—another artist who puts his version down. It's very exciting because you see the film growing.

Los Angeles or Hollywood in the West story is the place where American dreams of starting life all over again so often end in sadness. Looking at the film again recently, I found the Donald Sutherland character much more moving than I'd remembered. The character who's almost unre-

lievedly awful is the Karen Black one, the starlet, whom the
narrator lusts after.

I have lived to regret the casting of Karen Black, good
though she was. She played it very well, and she managed to
act the sort of artificiality of that extra that she was playing
without it appearing too artificial. I mean she inhabited that
character very thoroughly. The trouble was, she wasn't really
very attractive. She's not a great sex object, in my view, and I
feel there is an unsympathetic side to her personality, which I
didn't try to emphasize but it came through. We had readings
with various artists before we cast her. One was with Faye
Dunaway—and we read her very extensively. I don't know
why we came to the decision that she wasn't quite right.
There was something, perhaps, more raw about Karen Black.

Well, that comes through, and there is something sexy about
her in a trashy kind of way. Tod Hackett, the artist and nar-
rator of the story, played by William Atherton, is an edu-
cated man. Is his infatuation with her entirely sexual, or
does he recognize a kind of vulnerability?

I think it's a bit of both, because she isn't just sexual. If
we'd played that up, we should have cast someone much
more overtly sexual or prettier in a clichéd way. I could
imagine her in life being a bit birdbrained—hopping from
one thing to another, which is what she has to be.

The hardest thing must have been to get the character of the
narrator right, because he's not a very dramatic figure.

That was one of the problems of the script. There was no story, and we had to forge one, with a much stronger identity. So the story of the collapse of the set was something that affected Tod Hackett quite strongly. In the book it's not like that at all. We had to manufacture dramatic thrust where originally there was none, which resulted in the passing-of-the-buck scene in the barbershop, which wasn't there.

Apart from Robert Evans's misgivings, how was the film received when it was first shown?

I remember the first screening, which was a sort of preview of the film, which took place in Westwood. It was a packed house, and I got up very nervously in the middle and went out to the lobby because I didn't think it was going down very well, and Jerry Hellman met me there, and we both pulled a face and went for a coffee. Afterward, in a rather smart Italian restaurant in Beverly Hills, we found Polanski and Jack Nicholson, and a lot of people who were in *Chinatown,* sitting at the next table. They looked very embarrassed. Eventually someone came over and said, "I want to congratulate you," but they were obviously very embarrassed by their reaction—or lack of it—and so was I. I think the film generally wasn't being received terribly well.

The subject?

Well, it's possible, but you know, although I think it's one of the best pieces of writing about Hollywood, it wasn't popular as a book. It didn't have an enormous circulation or anything like that. I think there's an uncomfortable truth about it, which we succeeded in bringing out. It's certainly one of my better memories. Although I didn't get on with all of the actors, I just remember thinking at the time, "Oh, it's terrific, we're going off to work again," and I can't tell you how often that's not been the case.

HOLLYWOOD YEARS

═══

John Schlesinger never stopped trying to repeat the American success of *Midnight Cowboy*. The closest he came, in commercial terms, was *Marathon Man* (1976), adapted by William Goldman from his own novel. Starring Dustin Hoffman and Laurence Olivier, it was a beautifully executed genre movie—albeit a not very common genre, identified by John as "a Jewish thriller."

Yanks (1979) was a British film with an Anglo-American theme: affairs between British civilians and U.S. soldiers in World War II England. It was written by Colin Welland, and the cast included Vanessa Redgrave, Richard Gere, and William Devane. It won the David di Donatello Award and the Evening Standard British Film Award for best film.

After *Yanks* came the ill-fated *Honky Tonk Freeway* (1981), written by Edward Clinton. Considered by some as one of John's worst films and by others as a maligned classic,

Honky Tonk Freeway had a cast that included William Devane, Hume Cronyn, Jessica Tandy, and Beau Bridges.

Based on a true story about two privileged Californians spying for the Soviet Union, *The Falcon and the Snowman* (1985) was written by Steven Zaillian. The two stars were Timothy Hutton and Sean Penn.

When did you first come to America?

On tour, when I was a student acting in the Oxford University Dramatic Society. I suppose my interest in things American started then. I remember being taken by some hostess round the University of Chicago library and being told exactly how many volumes they had and how much they were worth but little else. The measuring of success by whether you had a second car in the garage or how many books the library held rather than what quality work there was, that was very marked to me.

The other thing that struck me was meeting people who had been uprooted. I was amazed by the fluid atmosphere in the country.

So many of your films are about dreamers and characters who try to reinvent themselves in one way or another. Does this have something to do with your fascination with the uprootedness of American society, the freedom it offers to remake yourself and start all over again?

I think it was also to do with the fact that for a long time I didn't feel I fitted in very comfortably anywhere. That's partly due, I suppose, to my sexual preference, and I found that wandering about the world was an answer to a lot of the questions that I had about where I belonged. I've always thought I wasn't terribly British in my interests and loyalties—not that I'm not critical of America, I am exceedingly so. I think the standards are very questionable.

In what way?

It seems to me there's a lot of energy that is devoted in pursuit of the mediocre.

You did a comedy about American dreams or selling American dreams, Honky Tonk Freeway *[1981]. It was not a success at the time—perhaps an underrated film. Yet it is not an unsympathetic view of America.*

No, I think you're right. It was never intended to be a savage satire, if it was a satire. It was affectionate. I love the idea of *Honky Tonk Freeway*—of all these people meeting one another on the road without really knowing when it was going to happen or why. That's one of the things about America I like. It's such an enormous question mark.

Your early British films were made on relatively modest budgets, compared to American movies. Later in your career you've taken on much more commercial Hollywood pictures, with very different challenges.

Yes. Which is why I think that the earlier part of my career, where I was taking bigger risks and tackling subjects that nobody else was tackling, was important. I don't look at some of my recent works and say: "Wow, that goes to the top of the class."

Why did you make that choice?

I don't know, really. I wanted to continue to work, and in order to do that I sometimes had to choose something that wasn't quite as personal to me as some of my earlier work. And if one was going to work within the studio system— whatever that might be—then commercial considerations in some way had to count. But if I'm asked to cite the films that I think worked best, they are the British films made for television. But since the offers came to do other stuff, I did it.

Was it almost impossible in the 1980s for a serious filmmaker to work in Britain and make the kind of films you wanted to do?

Probably, and I'm impatient. Things were more difficult to get off the ground, and therefore perhaps I was less obsessed with personal statement. Perhaps I made a mistake, I don't know.

When did you start having to sacrifice certain freedoms, such as having the right to the last cut?

I suppose it was when I started to make films like *Marathon Man*, where I was working for a studio. When I started to work for Paramount, they were all right, but I suffered the agonies of the previews and everybody having their say and "If you took a little less of that out, or put a little more of this in, you know, it would be better."

Surely a bad way to make movies?

Yes, it is. I don't like making movies by committee, but it doesn't mean to say the film won't work. *Marathon Man* is a film that I think succeeds.

How much interference was there in **Marathon Man** *[1976]?*

Only a bit. People expressed their opinions after a preview that hadn't gone well. I understand why previews exist, but they are dangerous because it's when you're at your most vulnerable as a filmmaker. You learn valuable things from previews, but they're still uncomfortable, because they encourage people to say too much against the film.

What was it that interested you about doing a thriller? You've tried your hand at it several times since. Was it the challenge of tackling a new kind of storytelling, or was it the story of **Marathon Man** *itself that attracted you—the New York Jewish student being persecuted by a Nazi war criminal and all that?*

There were all sorts of things that attracted me to the story. I always called it my Jewish thriller because that aspect of it was quite important. I remember asking Laurence Olivier whether it would be a good idea for him to grow a little mustache, and he said: "No, no, no. Don't you think you should use to the maximum my mean little mouth?" I could see his point. But there were many things I liked about *Marathon Man*, apart from the fact that I very much wanted to work with Robert Evans, the producer, who had said things that I didn't expect him to say after having seen *The Day of the Locust.*

What was the best thing about Evans?

Bob Evans was good on selling, which Joe Janni wasn't very interested in. He was interested in the design of advertising—he'd often call me into his office in years sub-sequently: "Come and look at the layout for the posters." I said: "How's the script?" "Oh, it doesn't matter about that. Come and look at the posters I've got." He was working on the selling, the promotion. He also had an extraordinary memory. He didn't come to one script conference. I was working on *Marathon Man* with Bill Goldman on my own. We were wandering around New York on Yom Kippur, and I said I would like to use this—the image of Jews rushing out, having a break from the shul, and rushing toward these burning vehicles. It had a sort of pertinence. So we were working on the script alone. But once we'd shot the film, and Bob was concerning himself with the editing, you've never seen a man so possessed with details—the right sound of the click of a broken neck when the Oriental man attacks Roy Scheider in his hotel room. All that kind of thing he wanted to get absolutely right—as I did, but I thought we were fuss-ing beyond belief.

But that was not necessarily a bad thing?

Oh, no, no. Not a bad thing—a very good thing. It's wonderful to find somebody who has got an attention to detail, whatever it may be.

The scene of Olivier being recognized by a former victim on Forty-seventh Street looks like something from a documentary film. How did you manage to shoot it among all the orthodox diamond dealers?

The camera is regarded in some places as the "evil eye," and I understand why. This is particularly true in orthodox Judaism. Since we were told that we couldn't produce a camera, since everybody would hide, we prepared a whole group of extras to walk into the street when Olivier appeared. In the event, the orthodox didn't hide at all. The real diamond merchants wanted to be in the picture, and we couldn't stop them from looking at the camera. So we had to close down and shoot the whole sequence on a Saturday, when of course there were no shops open.

Your mother often used to tell us about the time she visited you at your prep school, and you came tearing round a corner, pale with fear, being pursued by a bunch of schoolboy bullies. Clearly you're fascinated by persecution, mobs running amok, and by people being tortured. Persecution is a common theme in a lot of your work.

Persecution does terrify me. I can't imagine how someone can endure superhuman pain and fear and not give in, but it happens. I can't bear pain, and I don't really like seeing it inflicted on someone else. I don't really like the dark, I don't like weapons, I don't like insects, and I hate rats—but I've had them in several of my films because I think in a way it helps to exorcize the fear.

One thing that made **Marathon Man** *work is the way it combines violence and humor. Some of the cruelest scenes are also rather funny. For example, the torture scene.*

"Is it safe?" You mean, when Olivier keeps on repeating "Is it safe?" while working his drill?

Yes. And the sound of the drill is terrifying.

It's not comic, but I can see what you mean. It's tongue in cheek and macabre in the right way, which perhaps makes it laughable. Yes, I love all that. The cutting up of the body in *The Innocent* was something that also intrigued me greatly. That's why I admire Hitchcock so much, because he managed to find humor in so many different places. I wish I could do it better.

Doing thrillers?

I like doing thrillers, because it's a wonderful kind of game you play with an audience, because you've got to calculate in the telling of the story how much information to give the audience—trying not to show too much but just enough. You decide whether you want to give them a surprise or whether you want them to be saying as they're watching a scene, "Oh, don't do that," because they know something more, because you've let them into some sort of secret. It's great fun, because it is a game.

What was it like working with Laurence Olivier? He was a great stage actor. Was the transition from stage-acting to the cinema sometimes difficult for him? Did he have trouble with it?

I think he sometimes did. There's a compendium of rather bad performances by Olivier in the cinema, where things are overemphasized. I used to have to find a method of communication with him, which he'd understand but not be offended by. So I'd say: "Larry, do you think you could make this a little more intimate?" and he would say: "You mean cut off the ham fat?" and I said, "Precisely!"

So he was well aware of this failing?

Oh, yes, I think he was well aware of it, but Olivier was such a wonderful and admired actor that directors were sometimes frightened to say anything. They just let him have his head, and some of his performances are way over the top. There was a wonderful moment in *Marathon Man*, the final sequence, when he had a very long speech, which was lifted from the book, in which he said to Dustin Hoffman: "There are things that you must know about your brother. Your brother was a HOMOSEXUAL!" And it was sort of shouted out in such a hammy way that I had to cut it.

But I couldn't say: "Cut that, will you, Larry—it's terribly acted," so I told Dustin Hoffman not to move his eye line, and I knew where I could cut.

Here you had two actors coming from completely different traditions. What problems—if any—did that cause?

Olivier was from the school of "learn the role and don't deviate from it," so any cuts I had to make I had to make in my head and let him get on with it, knowing that some things were going to hit the cutting-room floor pretty fast. But Hoffman is an instinctive actor, who likes to be free and improvise. This can be very good, but it can also land you in problems, because it will go off the subject so easily.

As far as *Marathon Man* is concerned, Hoffman said that if he were to do the role, he wanted the character to be much less naïve. He said: "I can't be sexually naïve, I want to have had some experience, and therefore I don't want to be a student, I want to be a teacher." And we tried all these things—making him older—and I didn't think they worked. So in the end he was dissuaded, but I never thought he felt easy about it.

So he was quite difficult?

Yes. Hoffman was never satisfied that we'd gone far enough. He wouldn't trust me, so he wanted more takes, and he wanted to improvise scenes which he felt were too structured, and he felt hemmed in. It became rather boring.

But how did it work between Hoffman and Olivier, because Olivier didn't work like that? When Hoffman and Jon Voight improvised together, they were presumably more or less on the same wavelength. How did it work with a classical English actor?

Less well. Dustin is a great believer in physical acting. Whenever we had to do a running scene—you know, most actors would just say: "Well, just dab a bit of glycerine on my face, and I'll look sweaty." Not so with Dustin. He had to run right round the Ninety-first Street area of Central Park, so that he was really out of breath, which has always made me curious as to what they do when they're going to enact someone murdering somebody.

Or having sex.

Or having sex. Do they actually have to go through the motions? Sometimes they do, yes. We had to have a sauna by the side of the set, if there wasn't a place to run, so that Hoffman could sweat genuinely. It all wastes so much time.

How did the two actors approach the famous torture scene?

Olivier had worked out exactly how to say "Is it safe?" in a different way each time. I think he'd stood in front of the mirror and studied himself, and it was very effective. Hoffman's first reaction was: "I've got to look out of it, completely destroyed by pain." He thought he had to drink red wine or something much stronger to look out of it. I understand that, but I don't think that's the quickest or best means of getting a reaction. When I looked at the rushes of the scene, he certainly looked out of it, because he *was* out of it; there was no feeling in the eyes—they didn't move, nothing happened. And I thought, "Well, this is hopeless, I've got to reshoot Hoffman's close-ups again." When I told Olivier, he said very irritably: "Oh, why doesn't he just *act.*"

Did the differences between Olivier and Hoffman illustrate a more general difference between British and American actors? Are American actors still influenced by Actors Studio?

Oh, yes, I suppose they are. I went to the Actors Studio once in New York, and it infuriated me. They were doing a piece of *Macbeth,* and I can only describe it as a kind of hot-water acting. They were sitting round a hot tub, playing the Macduff scene, when the news of the murder of his wife and children is broken to him in England. They were sort of sitting on the edge of this so-called pool, dipping their fingers or their feet in, and going "Oooh." I didn't know what they were doing this for. I thought it was terrible. But I did work with Geraldine Page, who kept saying: "I'm obviously not feeling this right or thinking it right," and it made some sense to me. So the temptation to regard that church on the west side of New York as thoroughly pretentious wasn't always borne out.

The British do make a kind of pretense of the amateur spirit, don't they? Americans are more inclined to make a show of being overintense.

Well, Americans *are* intense, period. So why shouldn't it manifest itself in the Actors Studio? They take themselves very seriously and not always with humor. Hoffman's great thing was that he had an enormous sense of humor—he laughed at himself.

Did Jon Voight?

Jon Voight is also quite an intense actor. I remember when we were shooting a scene for *Midnight Cowboy* in New York, on Fifth Avenue, outside a bank. I wanted the bank vault to open, just as he was following a particular woman across the street. That's all I was really concerned about—the cuing. And as we were hiding in some airline office farther up the street, Voight sent a message with one of the assistants, asking: "What is my motivation?" And I sent a rather facetious reply: "A good fuck and plenty of dollars at the end of it." He was furious, didn't laugh at it at all, shook his fist—"If you ever do that to me again, I'll hit you." He became very intense, whereas you can imagine the Brits having a great emotional scene to play and making a joke in the wings before they go on. And I see no harm in that.

When you'd finished Marathon Man, *you did a film in England before returning to America again. It did have an American theme, though—Yanks [1979]. Were you looking*

*for projects in England, or was it just something that hap-
pened to come your way?*

No, Colin Welland, the writer of *Yanks*, who had worked
with Dustin before, came to visit us on the set of *Marathon
Man*. We were having a bad day. I felt we'd got what we
wanted, but Dustin wanted to improvise the scene and re-
tired to his dressing room in some state of disagreeableness.

Colin asked me whether I had ever thought of making a
film about the Americans in Britain during the war. And I
thought it was a marvelous idea. I loved the idea of that period: the sense of community, the singing at the organ in the
cinema, and all the other things that I remembered so well.
So the first thing we did was to advertise in a northern English paper for people who could tell us about their experiences with the Americans. And out of many replies came
this story of a woman who had had an affair with an American, which had gone all wrong. We based the story of *Yanks*
partly on her rather moving letter.

How much of your own memories went into the script?

Quite a lot, because we brought in an American writer to
help get the American side of things. Colin also despised the
idea of public school and upper-middle-class life. It wasn't
the happiest of collaborations.

*Yet Vanessa Redgrave's family, in the film, was very upper-
middle-class. And I found her relationship with the American officer the most interesting thing in the film. It had more*

depth than the affair between the younger couple, the one with Richard Gere.

I like Richard Gere and thought he gave a wonderful performance. But I liked the relationship between the easygoing American, played by William Devane, and this rather uptight upper-class woman, played by Vanessa Redgrave—she represented my mother a bit. I really was too young during the war to realize how lonely she must have felt and insecure. My father was away for four years in India.

Somehow the relationship between the two older people rings very true. It shows the mutual attraction between England and America—the Old World and the New—which nonetheless fails to connect at some level. And the younger couple, the English girl and her GI, have a failure at first but then come together in the final scene at the railway station.

They just catch a brief glimpse of each other waving over the railway bridge. There's no great love scene before to make everyone think that it's going to work in the end.

So both relationships are severed in the end?

Severed temporarily or maybe permanently. You see, I like making films that have question marks in them and are not all tied up beautifully with a pink ribbon, even though that's what the audience seems to want, and if you give it to them there's more assurance of commercial success, perhaps. But that's never the way I've seen life or reflected life in what I want to put on the screen.

You've lived much of your working life in America. Was Yanks *also a summing up of your feelings about the United States as compared to Britain?*

That was something I really wanted to explore, because by the time I made *Yanks* I'd spent a lot of time in America. I'd made two American films—*Midnight Cowboy* and *The Day of the Locust*—which were very particular of a period and the atmosphere of both New York and Los Angeles. I liked the idea of putting Britain and America together. *Yanks* has never been one of my favorite films—I don't know why—but I haven't seen it for a long time. I like to think that it shows the sort of stoicism of the British in wartime, which was a quality that was both admired and laughed at by the Americans, who in a sense had it all over the Brits.

I remember getting a letter from you when you were shooting The Falcon and the Snowman. *You wrote about the experience of working with a new generation of young American actors and how hard you were finding it. In what way were the younger actors different from the previous generation? Were they more brattish? They were clearly not less talented.*

No, not less talented. Brattish, certainly. Sean Penn was one of the stars in that film. Before starting the film, we met for lunch. He can be absolutely charming, and I thought:

"Oh, this is going to be fine. I've heard stories, but he's fine, and he's dead right for the part." And I got onto the subject of drugs and said: "Presumably, you know all about the taking of heroin and things like that?" And he said, Oh sure, there was no need to worry about that. We were rehearsing in Mexico. And because the actors came in groups from different places, the rehearsal period was scheduled very, very carefully and tightly. The Russians arrived from New York with the British actors, but there was no Sean Penn. We then discovered that he'd been on a heroin jag for several days. He arrived and said: "My God, what a trip that was!"

Was that in the same spirit as Dustin Hoffman having to have a real sweat, or was he a junkie?

No, he wasn't a junkie. Perhaps it was defiance toward me; it could well have been, because I've had problems since. I've got a theory that young actors—certainly young male actors—are vainer than women. They also like to create a stir around somebody they know to be gay, playing games with them, wanting me to in a way fall for them—which I certainly didn't. Also they have absolutely no respect for experience or opinions or anything like that. So it was difficult. I felt that I was being tested all the time.

Is this any different from the way actresses might behave toward heterosexual directors? Or do you think it's a slightly special situation?

I think it's a special situation.

Why?

I don't know why I think that, but I do. It's the natural thing for a director to become obsessed with his actors. So I can understand why there are so many cases of heterosexual directors falling in love with their leading ladies and possibly vice versa. But I don't think it's something that often happens to a gay director. That probably made a difference. I think any of these actors reading this will say: "Poppycock, ridiculous, how could I possibly have challenged JS in this way?" So I could be wrong.

But conversely, some gay directors have been extremely good at directing actresses. Is the lack of sexual tension possibly a help there?

Yes, I think that's absolutely true.

How did it affect the other actors, when somebody like Sean Penn would behave in an impossible manner?

Well, I used to get warnings from David Suchet, whom I adored. He always said the children need a lollipop. He would come and whisper to me when they were being rather late on the set: "I think you're going to have to distribute the lollipops, dear." And we'd talk in a kind of shorthand way that the Brits can do, with a certain amount of camp attached to it.

What was hardest thing about making this film?

Trying to shoot it in Mexico City. It's a terrible climate, and to shoot there constantly, six-day weeks, was really a chore. It became exhausting. The crew were just on their knees. So even though it affected me financially, because I had a deal in which I had to foot the bill if I went over budget, I said: "I'm sorry, I just can't go on. We must have a five-day week. We must have a weekend off."

But most of the interiors were presumably shot in Hollywood?

No, that would have been too expensive. They were all shot in Mexico, because the exchange rate and the costs made the budget manageable. It took us a long time to find the exterior of the Californian houses, which we had to do in Mexico. The only thing we were forced to shoot in Hollywood was the scene in a warehouse, where Daulton is tortured by the Mexican police after being caught—the dunking in the toilet bowl and all that sort of thing—because the Mexicans simply wouldn't allow us to show that that was what they did.

And you had to show the Mexicans what you were shooting?

Oh, we couldn't keep the censor away. There was a scene, for example, in which Sean Penn was snorting coke before he crossed a road. And I kept having to tell the executive producer: "Go and talk to the censor, keep her occupied." "But I've run out of things to say." "Well, just say anything but don't let her look at the shot that I'm taking."

So we couldn't show cruel treatment, otherwise she would have tried to stop it.

That scene is actually shot in a very interesting way, because what you see is the face of a man looking away from the torture.

Yes, I wasn't terribly interested in showing the detail of the torture—the thing is just to be aware of what is going on and of people, as it were, holding the strings, not looking.

You have said that one problem with The Falcon and the Snowman *is that the audience has nobody to root for. Two former altar boys from affluent Palos Verdes, who become Russian spies, one out of misplaced idealism, the other to impress. How could you have changed the problem of having no one to root for?*

By altering the truth, which is why I couldn't do it. I think the problems of audience identification were partly because the treachery of espionage is something that we laugh about in Europe more than in the United States. I mean, there's humor in the two Alan Bennett films about spies, which I made for the BBC. In *Falcon*, the cockamamie idealism of Chris Boyce, which he took seriously, made his act into something I could identify with. I don't condone what he did, which was treacherous, but I could recognize it as something worth studying, which made me want to do the film. You see, subjects for my films can come out of anywhere.

I wonder if the difference between the BBC films, An Englishman Abroad *[1983] and* A Question of Attribution *[1992], and* Falcon *lies in European and American attitudes to treachery. They are different kinds of spies, after all.* **The Falcon and the Snowman** *is about two callow kids, one of whom is a drug pusher. The other films are about two much older men, who had stopped being spies long ago.*

But I'm not sure if people living in England are really that much more sanguine about spying than Americans are.

Well, I wonder. I mean, we seem to have treated our classic spy stories with a certain amount of raised eyebrow and tongue in cheek—at least that's the way Alan Bennett saw it, I think, in those scripts.

Yes, there is a great deal of humor in Bennett's depictions of Blunt and Burgess, two camp gentlemen long past their prime. The characters of Boyce and Lee are less comical.

I think the humor came in the outrageousness of Daulton Lee's fantasy about being a spy. There was this enormous amount of fantasy associated with the theatricality of what he was going through. He was a loose cannon, and Boyce—who had at least a misplaced idealistic point of view—tried to put a brake on his once-upon-a-time friend. It was very difficult to do, because they are still living. Both of them were still in jail when we made the film. There were all sorts of problems that they faced if we did what the script intended to do. Even suggesting that Daulton Lee would wear a wire to help the police investigate a drug case could have landed him in terrible trouble in jail. He already faced enough as it was. So he, through Sean Penn, begged us to not tell that part of the story.

There is an element of fantasyland about the whole opera-tion of spying. This comes out very clearly in The Falcon and the Snowman. *There's Boyce sitting in this high-security place making cocktails using paper shredders, and at one point I think he says to his interrogators that they are all Keystone Kops. Which is similar to Anthony Blunt's famous remark to his interrogators that it was all about "cowboys and Indians, cowboys and Indians." I don't know if it's in your film* A Question of Attribution.

It isn't in the film.

He said it in real life, which was a little disingenuous be-cause the consequences of what he did were more serious. But there is certainly that farcical element.

Yes, which is why I was interested.

Boyce's last speech. Was it the intention of the scriptwriter and yourself to somehow make his behavior seem, if not ad-mirable, then at least more understandable, by showing what a dirty game the Americans were playing?

Yes. That was precisely what we were all thinking. This was Steve Zaillian's first script to be made into a film. He is a brilliant writer and a serious man. And I kept going on about how this was the only place where we could make the audience feel that there was some justification, however fucked-up it was in his head, for what he had done. I don't believe it was playacting, as it was in Daulton Lee's case. There was a misplaced feeling of genuine outrage.

When we watched the tape of the film together you said you found the ending unsatisfactory. Why?

There are no surprises in the storytelling. They're arrested, they're coming down the corridor, they're seen by the families, which I think would have been impossible, but I wanted to make it dramatic, having them carted off in full view. I don't know what surprise we could have had, but just to see them in chains—contrasted with the flight of the falcon, just whirling around freely—it's too pat. I wished we'd had a better idea, put it that way. It goes on too long and says the same thing.

You've worked with all the advantages of the Hollywood system. Can one become addicted to big budgets at the expense, perhaps, of personal autonomy?

I don't think I've ever had an unlimited budget. I've gone over budget quite often. *Midnight Cowboy* did. We produced a budget of $2.8 million, which is chicken feed compared to today. Although some of my films were referred to as "Hollywood productions," they're not Hollywood in the way that the word implies—they're not lavish. Not all of them. I'm trying to think when I have ever had unlimited money to spend. I don't think ever.

Fassbinder and other independent directors always had to work fast and cheaply. Do you think this might have had its advantages?

I've gone backward and forward between television and the big screen, though I don't like television on principle, because I don't think you have the full attention of the audience. But I have learned a great deal about short cuts. I think it makes you think of ways of telling a story in a simpler way, perhaps. On the other hand, if you look at *Madame Sousatzka*, there's a lack of bigger shots, because they would have cost too much. This may have mitigated against the film. I don't know. I do like a show, I must confess.

TOWARD THE END

The last decade of John's career yielded some of his best, as well as his most questionable, work. The best films were made for British television. *An Englishman Abroad* (1983), based on a true story about the spy Guy Burgess and written by Alan Bennett, was made for the BBC and starred Alan Bates as Burgess and Coral Browne as herself. It won five British Academy Awards, a Broadcasting Press Guild Award, and the best fiction film award at the Barcelona Film Festival.

Alan Bates also starred, with Julie Christie and Claire Bloom, in another film made for television (ITV and HBO), *Separate Tables* (1983), adapted from Terence Rattigan's play.

The Believers (1986), written by Mark Frost, starring Martin Sheen, was a low point in John's career. This competently directed story about black magic in New York City is best forgotten.

A much better film is *Madame Sousatzka* (1988), written by Ruth Prawer Jhabvala and starring Shirley MacLaine, Peggy Ashcroft, and Shabana Azmi.

John made another thriller, *Pacific Heights,* in 1990, written by Daniel Pyne and starring Mathew Modine, Melanie Griffith, and Michael Keaton. It was shot in San Francisco and Los Angeles.

John directed his first opera production, *The Tales of Hoffmann,* in 1980, at the Royal Opera House in London. This won the Society of West End Theatre Award. *Der Rosenkavalier* followed at the Royal Opera House in 1984. He directed *The Masked Ball* for the Salzburg Festival in 1989.

In 1992 came *A Question of Attribution*, the second Alan Bennett film play for the BBC about a British spy. Anthony Blunt is played by James Fox, and Queen Elizabeth by Prunella Scales. This, as well as *An Englishman Abroad* and *Cold Comfort Farm* (1995), adapted from the Stella Gibbons novel, made up in quality for the relative decline shown in some of John's late Hollywood pictures. Leading actors in *Cold Comfort Farm* included Eileen Atkins, Kate Beckinsale, and Ian McKellen. *A Question of Attribution* won the British Academy Award for best single TV drama.

In 1994 John directed *The Innocent,* adapted from his own novel by Ian McEwan. Shot on location in Berlin, the leading roles were played by Anthony Hopkins and Isabella Rossellini.

Eye for an Eye (1996), starring Sally Field and Ed Harris, is a well-directed revenge story. The script is by Amanda Silver and Rick Jaffa.

His last film made for television, *The Tale of Sweeney Todd* (1998), written by Peter Buckman and Peter Shaw, featured Ben Kingsley as the murderous barber.

John's last feature film, *The Next Best Thing* (2000), was written by Tom Ropelewski and starred Madonna and Rupert Everett.

He won a Directors Guild of Great Britain lifetime achievement award in 2002. He was too ill to attend the ceremonies in Los Angeles and London.

John died on July 25, 2003, in Palm Springs, California.

Madame Sousatzka *was your last British feature film. What drew you to the story of a young piano prodigy? Was it the musical theme?*

I keep forgetting that that was my last British film. It wasn't terribly well thought of, but I'm proud of it and enjoyed making it. I think what drew me to the story was, in a sense, what I was going through. Opportunity, commercialism, and the perhaps rather old-fashioned approach of the music teacher, Sousatzka, who won't let her pupil perform before he's absolutely ready. It's about artistry, and I took that very seriously. Those were themes that were personally interesting to me. The film was made on a smallish budget, and we didn't have the resources to open it up a bit more, which I would like to have done. It's about music, too, of course. But, you see, I don't have a great backlog of stuff about which I say: "Ooh, I must make a film about this or I must make a film about that." I don't function that way. I'm much more intuitive.

Yet music always held a great attraction. You have directed several operas.

I actually did a musical, called *I and Albert*, about Queen Victoria and her Consort, before I ever went and did an opera production. It was an interesting idea because it was like making a film onstage. We had forty back projectors and a lot of Victorian frames as screens for photographs. It wasn't realistic, it was stylized. A room in Buckingham Palace, for example, would be represented by a piece of blown-up wallpaper— that's all you saw of it.

It was very fascinating to do, but the problem was that everybody was pulling in different directions. We had an American book writer, who was the wife of one of the producers, and they seemed to me to be terribly sentimental about royalty, as the Americans are. And then we had Charlie Strouse and Lee Adams, who were well-known composers of musicals, working together on the score. They'd write some of their stuff in the nosh bar opposite the Windmill Theatre. If I found a particularly embarrassing and flowery speech in the text, to which I rather objected, I went up to them having their chopped liver or whatever and asked them to do some pruning. They'd say: "Oh, yes, sure, it'll be better." But then the book writer would see it and protest that a whole speech had been cut. It was difficult. I understand why people say, "Where would Hitler be if he was alive today?" The answer being: "On the road with a Broadway musical!"

He would have been quite good at it.

I should think so.

That was the only musical you've done?

Yes, I wanted desperately to do the film of *Fiddler on the Roof,* but I'd had a flop with *Far from the Madding Crowd,* and so I didn't get it.

Why that particular musical?

I like the musical as a piece of work. It was all so Jewish, too. That points in its favor, and it was sad and funny and touching—qualities that I wanted the audience to feel. But I didn't get it, Norman Jewison did.

Still, I think the opera world became available to me as a result of doing *I and Albert.* I remember one of the critics—and maybe more than one—saying: "This man should be doing opera," and I did, and very, very exciting it was. Terrifying, but wonderful.

How soon after I and Albert *did you do your first opera?*

Oh, some years later. I was going to do *Carmen* with Placido Domingo. But then I saw a production of *Carmen* which seemed to answer all the questions I might have had. So I decided not to bother. *Sunday Bloody Sunday* was due to be made anyway. We had the script by that time, so it must have been the early seventies. And Domingo said: "You will regret it, if you never do an opera, and I'd love to do an opera with you."

And eventually you did.

Yes, *Tales of Hoffmann* [1980]. It was very successful and enjoyable and theatrical—fantasy and reality again. And it's still in the repertory. They revived it quite recently.

What special problems did you face, producing opera for the first time?

I suppose the sheer problems of working with singers, of knowing that you've got so many bars of music to get someone on or off stage and paying great attention to musical cues. But *Hoffmann* is not full of musical themes representing characters. It doesn't have the leitmotifs that you have in a Wagner opera, which I've never done, or in *Rosenkavalier*, which I did do four years later, where there's specific music meant for a character. In *Rosenkavalier* I had to hurry part of the opera to sync the correct music up with an entrance of the main character. It's possible to have new ideas and try to make them work, without having to do a disservice to the composer and the librettist. But *Rosenkavalier* was a big pill, because I don't speak German. My agent said I had to learn German to do it, but I didn't bother and found myself in deep shit when I came to rehearsal.

Because of the language?

Yes, not only should you speak German but you should know how to cope with the Viennese idiom, too. So I wouldn't do that again.

Didn't you want to do, and even prepare to do, Salome at one time?

Yes, I was going to do *Salome* with a wonderful singer, Anja Silja, who objected to the art-nouveau costume. She wanted to wear the costume designed for her by her lover, Wieland Wagner.

You wanted to do a sort of Aubrey Beardsley version of Salome?

Yes, much more than she did. So there was implacable resistance from early on. And I used to talk about my conception of the opera, and her agent said: "Don't talk about conception—she doesn't want to know!" So that was it. I didn't do it.

A pity.

Yes, I don't know if I'd want to go with Aubrey Beardsley now. It seems rather obvious. But it is an exotic opera, and I'd done the Oscar Wilde play. I'd been in it as First Jew.

When was this?

Oh, God, it was years ago.

How big was the part of First Jew?

Not very big. A great friend of mine, Noel Davis, played a similar minor part, and we were out to steal the scene from each other. Even though the costumes had been designed, we wanted more glitter, so we both went out independently and bought yards more gold or silver lamé and added it to our costumes and made suitable sounds when Salome was dancing, exposing the operation scars round her belly. We would go "AAAAAh" in what I hope was a suitable example of our lust for her body. Anyhow, that was that.

You did **Un Ballo in Maschera** *with Herbert von Karajan. What was it like to work with him?*

Oh! It was absolutely fascinating! I didn't want to get into deep water. When he wanted to discuss how people accused him of being a Nazi and all that type of thing, I should have said: "Well, then how come you have this reputation of being so monstrous?" But I couldn't bring myself to speak that candidly.

Or ask him what he was doing in the SS . . .

I could have done, but I didn't. Everybody held him in awe, of course. I wasn't actually frightened of him, but I was frightened of the idea of working with him. Originally, he asked me to do a production of *Boris Gudunov* with Claudio Abbado conducting. So I went to Vienna, and I was given about five minutes with the maestro—Abbado, that is. I thought he treated me appallingly for someone who'd come especially to see him. And he obviously didn't want me to do *Boris.* I flew back to London that afternoon, and Karajan was told of what had happened and was absolutely furious. I didn't mind the fact that Abbado didn't want me to do it, but I was interested in Karajan's reaction, which was very, very angry. Then he asked me to do *Tosca* with him, but the sets had already been designed, and I didn't really want to come in as a sort of assistant. I wanted to have a say in the conception of the whole thing. So I didn't do that and thought I'd shot my bolt. And then he proposed *Un Ballo in Maschera,* which was going to be a totally original design. He was present at every rehearsal and showed that he had an enormous sense of humor—it was rather black. In the Ulrika scene, he said: "Vat are you doing viv those vomen looking upstage at this moment? They are bitches, they will turn round and ruin the whole thing. They are bitches, I know!" So I said that if we told them not to turn round, perhaps they wouldn't. "No, I know them—they are bitches!"

You came out in public as a homosexual in the 1980s. You have said it was impossible to come out earlier. What were the constraints in Hollywood in the 1960s and 1970s? How damaging would it have been?

I really can't say. All I know is that George Cukor, who was a friend, once told me that he could never have lived as Michael and I lived, as a couple, in the forties.

But when you had those discussions that was already, what, in the seventies?

Yes.

You were in a privileged profession. . . .

And it's not exactly homophobic, by and large.

Not like working in a bank.

No, exactly. And so if it's going to help people in a less privileged position, who are uncomfortable with their sexual orientation and extremely unhappy with their lives, and if it's going to encourage somebody to say, "Well, look at him, he's done all right, why shouldn't I?" then I think it's an important thing to do.

Were there any repercussions or any reactions that made you feel that there was a price to pay?

No, some people said: "Oh, God, you're so brave to have done what you've done" and that sort of thing or "It's such a risk"—and maybe it is, I don't know. I know of no statement from anyone or any studio executive saying: "I don't know if we can entrust this film to him. He's come out." I suppose one of the disadvantages is that with open discussions of AIDS, there are people who might be very shocked by the publicity over what the homosexual community has got up to. Too many details have been spread about, which I wish hadn't.

Details?

Sexual activities.

Bathhouses and that kind of thing?

Well, more than that. I mean the subject has come up so that people who would not really have been interested or curious about what we got up to during the heady days of the sixties and seventies may well have been made more aware and put off by overt descriptions of sexual practices, which they didn't need to know.

I don't think that AIDS did cause more homophobia, though. On the contrary, there was quite a lot of rallying around.

Yes, there was rallying around. And I think the gay community behaved in an extremely encouraging fashion, by taking their plight into their own hands and organizing all kinds of things, charities, and so on.

Have you ever had any interest in being an activist like Larry Kramer, to be involved in the politics of it all?

No. Because I'm not really a political animal. I feel ambivalent about people acting up and making a fuss in the

House of Commons. I don't think that's the best way to get change done. My view is: For God's sake don't frighten the horses. Change is absolutely essential, but there's a way of handling it, and I don't know that confrontation is necessarily going to do it.

Sometimes you need confrontation.

Yes, sometimes you do. But I don't think all the time.

To what extent is being gay still a problem in Hollywood if you're an actor?

Oh, I think it's an enormous problem for actors, terribly.

Still?

Oh, yes.

But not for directors?

I suppose, you know, information is power. I don't know who's opposed my name going forward toward a project. They're certainly not breaking down the doors, but I'm not breaking down their doors to work necessarily. I really only have the energy—if I have it—to do something I'm absolutely, ravenously committed to, artistically rather than financially.

Perhaps every director has at least one great unmade film. Yours would surely be Hadrian VII, **the play based on the**

*novel by Frederick Rolfe, or Baron Corvo. The story of a
kind of Billy Liar figure with fantasies of becoming the
pope was almost made for you to do.*

Oh, yes, and I'd still like to do it. We've redone the script
recently.

So it's not dead?

No, but I think it would be very difficult in the present
climate.

It has all your themes. A dreamer . . .

An impossible outsider . . .

So what went wrong?

I think people just didn't understand the script, because
we doubled parts. The king of Italy is also the publisher who
rejects the main character as an author.

Who wrote the script?

Charles Wood. He is still working on it, or was.

But what was the problem?

Couldn't get it financed. It was a Columbia picture, and
Columbia passed on it on Christmas Eve—one of the most
depressing Christmases I ever had.

Alec McCowen was going to play Hadrian?

Yes. And then for a period I'm afraid I was disloyal to
Alec and went to Dustin Hoffman. He wanted to test for

the part, which we did. I don't know if he'd seen the play or not, but he loved the idea of it. If he could have coped with the English accent, it might have been OK. Anyhow, we did a test, and he was going back to America and wanted to see the test with his manager, who may have been a boxing promoter or something of that sort. On the morning of seeing the test I had an accident with my coffeepot. I bent too far over the coffeepot and the plunger went in and very, very hot coffee went into my face. So I was delayed from getting to the theater to see the test, and Dustin had to see them alone with his manager. And I think his manager talked him out of doing it because he felt it was too uncommercial.

But it was a great success as a play?

Yes, but that doesn't guarantee anything. A successful play is not necessarily seen as a commercial movie. I wished it had been. We had all sorts of ideas. The studio financed a trip to Italy with Tony Walton as the designer to look at certain places that we could make work. In the end I think it would have worked if we'd made St. Pancras Station into the Vatican.

That would have been great.

Then we decided to design it in such a way that his room would reflect what he was imagining as he was writing. You know, the Sistine Chapel much decorated by his own hand with rather irreverent drawings. Still, it was not to be.

You have also tinkered with ideas to do a film based on our family. There has been quite a lot of drama in the family. The suicide of your youngest sister, my Aunt Susan, for example. Did you ever think of using such things in your work?

I haven't used it yet, but I may if I make another movie. I remember very well going to see Grandma Schlesinger when she was dying—she was lying in bed making funny noises and things like that, which were disturbing. My parents were there, and they told me to go over to my other grandmother, who lived in the next block of flats. So I went to see her and waited for the phone call.

And you used that in a film?

No. But I did use the sound in *Billy Liar*—the sort of "uuh, uuh, uuh," sort of childlike sounds that Grandma Schlesinger was emitting.

When you are experiencing things that are very distressing, are you aware that part of your mind is always working, always thinking: "How can I use that?"

I've been very conscious of things that I've seen or experienced or heard and said: "That's interesting—I think I could use that." In a way this puts a barrier between yourself and the event, whatever that might be.

I think it was Graham Greene who once said that there was a sliver of ice running through the heart of every novelist.

Yes. The other day I was watching our beloved dog being put to sleep and observing the details of it, how quickly it happens, and it helps to put a barrier between emotion and the event, because you are.... I don't know how I'd use it, but I did wonder whether, if it was so easy to stop a dog's heart beating, that would work on a human being. A lethal injection is less dramatic than hanging, but there are all sorts of stories about how it can go wrong.

You have often shown the routine mechanics of people going about their work—even if it's grotesque work. And it is often rather funny. There is a scene in a morgue in one of your films, perhaps even more than one. And in An Englishman Abroad *you see the shoemaker blowing dust off models of people's feet, people who have been long dead.*

Of course, that scene is made even more extraordinary by actually seeing a man trying on a pair of boots that have been made for him—and it turns out to be a recognizable person in the shape of Emperor Bokassa, about whom there were all sorts of rumors about what he did with children and the fridge.

About the sort of things that turned up in his fridge.

Yes. And there he was, looking very civilized with a beautiful stick with an embossed handle, trying on his shoes while we were about to shoot.

You are not a particularly religious man. But you use religion a lot in your films, although there seems to be a difference between your British movies and your American ones. In some of the British films—I'm thinking of the end of Yanks, *for example, or* Far from the Madding Crowd—*the people singing in churches suggest a rooted community of people conforming to convention, to tradition. In the American films, religion is treated more satirically—the world of television evangelists, a bit theatrical and rather crazy.*

Well, I love the difference in that. I wouldn't describe myself as a religious person, but I do feel tradition very strongly in Britain and therefore want to express it. There are certainly two—if not more—church scenes in *Yanks.*

Yes, and then there's the synagogue scene in Sunday Bloody Sunday, *which clearly shows a certain devotion to tradition.*

Yes, which emphasizes—I hope—the feeling of the gay doctor, who doesn't conform. I don't say it worries him, but it certainly brings back memories of his youth, of going up in front of everybody and speaking his portion in the Bar Mitzvah service. I like both tradition and the breaking of it, because it says something about the people in the film, and that's very important to me.

In The Day of the Locust, *religion is almost a variation of the Tinseltown that you see in the movies. It's almost a form of entertainment, of deluding the public. It's trying to capture an audience by promising miracles and selling itself in the way that films do.*

To a certain extent I think of all organized religion as a con trick.

In The Day of the Locust *it is overtly so. Religion in most of your American films comes across as a con trick. But my point is that that's not the way you use religion in your British films.*

Yes. But one doesn't necessarily think of this intellectually when one's working on a script. It's often entirely intuitive.

It's what works in the context of a particular story?

Quite often it's something that pops into the mind when you're preparing a movie—the choice of location and everything else, combined with what you're trying to say about the story and the people in the story.

But the reason I find this interesting is because crossing the Atlantic and back is a constant theme in your life and work. So yes, everything is chosen to fit the story you're filming. But perhaps you look at America differently from the way you look at the country you grew up in. After all, there are

many American films, made by Americans, which also
stress community and tradition. You were saying yourself
how you were interested in the mobility and the flux, the up-
rootedness of the place.

Oh, I am. I am interested in that because it's something
that I don't think I could live my life enduring. I like roots,
which is why I could never give up partly living in Britain.
I'm so used to moving around, even in Los Angeles itself,
where I live in rented apartments and houses. But I like
coming home to my own place and the familiarity of my
own things.

Do you still go to synagogue because you believe, or is it
more about continuity and tradition?

I think its probably the latter, because I don't observe the
dietary rules of orthodox Judaism. My grandmother, who
worshipped in the liberal synagogue, as we all did, observed
them. We used to tease her terribly. Hold up our pieces of
bacon—crisp and smelling good—and say: "Come on,
Grandma, do try it—you'll regret it if you don't." She'd always refuse.

But she was married to an orthodox husband, whom our
cousin Marjorie Schwab described as very German.

She said that? I used to borrow her mother's dressing
gown, when I used to go and see her family, while I was in
the army. Marjorie's mother was very striking. I used to go

and have baths there, and since I had nothing to wear she would lend me her dressing gown. I tried to wrap it around my bulk.

Who was the relative, the actor, who always fell on his face in the play Charley's Aunt?

That was Maurice. Maurice Ellinger, whom I used in one or two films. He was an amusing man, always covered in a mess of snuff spilled down his front, and seemed to me to be using the pub as a money-lending place. I loved this extraordinary family. They were colorful. Desiree, who was an opera singer, sang in the Beecham opera company, in the early thirties in Covent Garden.

Was she the one who always complained that her rings were too heavy?

Did she? She was a very good-looking woman. She got ill but still wanted to sing, and she would have a friend push her in a wheelchair up to the BBC studio door and then get out and walk, so she continued to be employed. She would never let you in to see her until the full makeup had been applied. I sometimes visited her in her apartment, near Marble Arch, and you would hear: "Just a second, won't be a minute." There was a theatricality about a lot of my family. My uncle, my mother's brother, was a judge. The court is of course a very dramatic place. I sat on the bench with him sometimes, at West Ham. He was very lenient with good-looking young men.

He was a frustrated theatrical figure. In fact, didn't he once act with John Gielgud?

He did but not professionally. He was a great friend of a character actor who created the part of Mole in *The Wind in the Willows*, which was dramatized as a popular Christmas entertainment, and he played it for years. "Oh my, oh my . . ." I can remember the voice. "Oh my, oh my . . . oh my, oh my . . ."

These were the last coherent sentences that I have on tape. We had agreed to meet again in Palm Springs. But before we did, John suffered a stroke, which paralyzed him on one side and made speech difficult. I visited him soon after, and there were conversations of a kind. A remembered movie, a salacious anecdote—these occasionally pricked his interest enough to produce a response. I would wheel him around his garden, and he would give me short, whispered instructions: "More to the left . . . to the right . . . stop here. . . ."

He wanted to give it another try. We sat down, beside the pool, a mike attached to his shirt, the tape recorder running. I asked him what he would like to talk about. After a long pause, he whispered the name of his first producer, Joe Janni. What about him? He thought for a while, trying to find the words. But he couldn't.

We tried once again the following day. I asked him whether his illness had made him reflect on his life's work. Yes, he said, yes it had. What had he been thinking about? And yet again the words wouldn't come. At last, one word:

"Sexuality." Did he mean sexuality in his films? "Yes." What about sexuality? Had he not explored it far enough? "Not far enough."

It was difficult to know what he meant precisely. Perhaps he felt that he should have continued on the path of *Sunday Bloody Sunday* and made more personal films, probing the borders of his favorite subject, the different kinds of human relationships. This is almost certainly why—apart from hoping for a final Hollywood hit—he decided to embark on his last film, *The Next Best Thing*. The subject of a gay man trying to be a father did appeal to him. I would have loved to have pursued this topic with him further, but the words simply were not there.

Perhaps it was just as well that we ended our conversation where we did. His memory of an actor playing Mole in *The Wind in the Willows* had the mixture of humor, theatricality, and whimsy that was typical of him. I don't think he would have wanted to finish on a more abstract, more analytical note. That would have smacked of the way "intellectuals" talked. A wistful joke suited him better.

It suited the humanism of his best films, too. There are aspects of *Midnight Cowboy, Billy Liar, Darling*, or *Sunday Bloody Sunday* that might seem dated now—political references, cinematic styles, social attitudes—but the humanity, observed by an artistic eye that was both compassionate and sharp and always humorous, will endure. Once seen, the characters are hard to forget: the Jewish doctor in *Sunday Bloody Sunday*, the go-getting Diana in *Darling*, Billy, Joe

Buck and Ratso. John did not invent these characters, but he made them come alive on the screen in a way that only the greatest directors can do.

John knew his gifts but also his limitations. He often said, not as a lament but as a matter of fact, that he was not an innovator in the way Fellini was or Godard or Buñuel. More than these directors, he relied on the writing of others. And yet he did have a style that was instantly recognizable, even in his least successful films. It is a combination of operatic flair and documentary observation that is exceedingly rare, a kind of dramatic realism, which, when it works, is exhilarating. The fact that it did not always work is regrettable, perhaps, but also a sign that he was not afraid to take risks. He always insisted that an artist must be prepared to risk failure. Total consistency is almost always the mark of mediocrity.

Things got worse after his second stroke. For a time, he didn't say anything at all but simply stared ahead, physically alive but all but gone. Words came back later, to some extent, and then faded away again. He died in July 2003. I miss him, as the perfect bachelor uncle, as a wise counselor when needed, as one of the funniest, wickedest storytellers I ever knew, as a coconspirator of fun. But we are still left with his films, the testament to his enduring humanity.

ACKNOWLEDGMENTS

One of the worst chores for a book like this is transcribing the taped interviews. I was largely relieved of this burden by John's secretary, Isabel Macdonald, and my sister, Ann Buruma.

The interviews in Palm Springs could not have taken place without the excellent and loving care taken of John by Maureen Dansman.

I am grateful for Michael Childers's permission to use his photographs. Roger and Sue Schlesinger kindly allowed me to look for material at John's old country house in Sussex.

In preparing this book I have had the benefit of a patient editor in Julia Cheiffetz, and an always supportive agent, Jin Auh of the Wylie Agency.

ABOUT THE AUTHOR

IAN BURUMA is a writer and journalist. His books include *Wages of Guilt, Bad Elements, Anglomania,* and *Occidentalism.* He is a professor at Bard College and lives in New York City.